Praise for

THE ART OF
EXECUTION

*"I am often asked by graduate students what books I have read that I could recommend
they read to make the students better investors. My answer generally is that the student
should read* The Intelligent Investor *and* Reminiscences of a Stock Operator;
I have now added this book to the list ... I wish I had read it 30 years ago!"

DENNIS M. BRYAN
PARTNER, FPA FUNDS

*"This book makes a very good point ... the person who knows his character, and is
knowing of his environment and his investment horse, is the one that wins over the long
term, provided that he is asked to make defined decisions."*

CRISPIN ODEY
FOUNDING PARTNER, ODEY ASSET MANAGEMENT

*"Provides a comprehensive framework for how to deal with losing positions and how to
make winning positions have a big positive impact on your portfolio returns. A great read
for investment novices and professionals alike."*

DIRK ENDERLEIN
PARTNER AND FUND MANAGER, WELLINGTON

*"Invaluable lessons for both the private and professional investor ... lays bare the
behavioural pitfalls we are all subject to in executing our investment ideas."*

JAMES INGLIS-JONES
FUND MANAGER, LIONTRUST

*"The insights are terrific and it will serve as an internal voice of conscience forcing me to
scrutinise execution and timing more thoroughly."*

DANIEL NICKOLS
FUND MANAGER AND HEAD OF UK SMALL AND MID-CAP EQUITIES,
OLD MUTUAL GLOBAL INVESTORS

THE ART OF
EXECUTION

How the world's best investors get it wrong
and still make millions

LEE FREEMAN-SHOR

HARRIMAN HOUSE LTD

18 College Street
Petersfield
Hampshire
GU31 4AD
GREAT BRITAIN
Tel: +44 (0)1730 233870

Email: enquiries@harriman-house.com
Website: www.harriman-house.com

First published in Great Britain in 2015.

Paperback ISBN: 978-0-85719-495-4
eBook ISBN: 978-0-85719-502-9

British Library Cataloguing in Publication Data
A CIP catalogue record for this book can be obtained from the British Library.

For my son, Adam, and my wife, my soul mate, Michal.

I am truly blessed to be your father and husband respectively. I love you both more than words on a page can convey.

To my Mum and Dad, who are quite simply the best parents a son could wish for. I got lucky in life.

About the author

Lee Freeman-Shor currently manages over $1bn in high-alpha and multi-asset strategies. Lee was ranked as one of the world's top fund managers in Citywire 1000 in 2012. He has been AAA-rated by Citywire, Gold-rated by S&P Capital IQ fund research and is Bronze-rated by Morningstar OBSR. He has been at Old Mutual Global Investors since October 2005 and was previously Co-Head of Equity Research.

Prior to joining Old Mutual Global Investors, Lee worked for Schroders, Winterthur and in private client wealth management and has over 16 years' investment experience. Lee holds the Investment Management Certificate and has an LLB (Hons) Law degree from Nottingham Trent University. He currently lives in Maidenhead, England, with his wife Michal and their son Adam. In his spare time he enjoys going to the movies and having fun with his family.

CONTENTS

INTRODUCTION

"I hope you weren't planning on a long career in the investment industry."

My colleague gave me a look of concern as he finished reviewing my research – an investigation into the performance of some of the very best City and Wall Street investors.

"Make sure you double check your findings," he continued. "If they're correct, you have made a discovery that will shock the public and make waves throughout the financial world."

I double-checked my findings. The results were confirmed. This book was born.

THE 'WOW' MOMENT

Over a period spanning more than seven years, from June 2006 to October 2013, I examined 1,866 investments, representing a total of 30,874 trades made by 45 of the world's top investors – all of whom I had the privilege of managing as part of my job as a fund manager at Old Mutual Global Investors.

What was unique about these 1,866 investments was that each one of them represented the best money-making ideas of these investment titans during those seven years.

I had given each of these leading investors between 20 and 150 million dollars to invest for my Best Ideas fund, with strict instructions that they could only invest in ten stocks that represented their very best ideas to make money.

The rationale for doing so was the simple belief that the greatest possible returns on capital could be achieved by hiring the best investors in the world and getting them to invest in their best ideas.

These were ideas that they had significant confidence in, and were often the result of hundreds of hours of research by some of the smartest people on the planet.

Given all this, I was sure that I would make a lot of money.

It might surprise you, then, to be told that most of their investments *lost* money.

WHEN THE BEST FAIL

Personally, I was shocked to discover that only 49% (920 investments) of the very best investment ideas made money.

Even more shocking was that some of these legendary investors were only successful 30% of the time.

I had employed some of the greatest investment minds on the planet and asked them to invest in only their very best, highest-conviction, money-making ideas. And yet the chances of them making money were worse than tossing a coin and betting on heads coming up every time.

"[A]fter studying forecasting day and night for over 30 years ... I've yet to find anyone who could consistently and reliably forecast an uncertain future."[1]

– Ned Davis

What really surprised me wasn't the discovery that so many investing legends – earning tens of millions every year and appearing in annual rich lists – had feet of clay. What really fascinated me was the fact that, despite some of them only making money on one out of every three investments, overall *almost all of them did not lose money*. In fact, they still made a lot of it.

This begged the question:

How are they making lots of money if their ideas are wrong most of the time?

How are most of these investment legends able to be wrong more often than they are right and still make incredible profits?

What was the secret of their success if it wasn't down to an elusive Midas touch?

This question made me burn with curiosity. It led me to analyse every single trade they had made over a seven-year period to try and uncover their secrets. I simply had to know what it was they did.

The results of my investigation are revealed in this book.

In the process I discovered that successful stock market investing is not about being right *per se* – far from it. Success in investing is down to how great ideas are executed.

I have come to understand that if successful property investing is all about 'location, location, location', success in equity investing is all about 'execution, execution, execution'.

"Vision without execution is hallucination."
– Thomas Edison

I have also learned that investing need not be the preserve of the so-called experts. Until now, the skill of good execution in investing has been largely hidden from the general public. This has led to a widespread false belief that great investors are great because they have ideas that at the time elude the rest of us mere mortals.

This couldn't be further from the truth. It is why this book has been carefully written to have appeal to investors of every level, both private and professional; no specialist knowledge is required.

As you will see later in the book, you don't even have to worry about whether an investing idea works or not if you focus on *how* to invest in that idea: how much money you allocate to it and what you will do when you find yourself in a losing or winning position.

Of course, in some ways I am not the first person to discover this.

Leo Melamed, the pioneer behind financial futures, once said: "I could be wrong 60% of the time and come out a big winner. The key is money management."

Likewise, legendary billionaire hedge fund manager Paul Tudor Jones II – a man who made his fortune from investing – is reported to have said that "the reason for all the Wall Street success stories he knew was down to: money management, money management, money management".[2]

And George Soros – a similar self-made billionaire trader – once pointed out that:

> "It's not whether you're right or wrong that's important, but how much money you make when you're right and how much you lose when you're wrong."

What is different about this book is that, for the first time ever, I have detailed *evidence* of how investment titans go about their money management.

I know what their secrets are. And soon you will too.

HOW THIS BOOK IS STRUCTURED

My findings show that the key to successfully executing great ideas and making lots of money comes down to the actions you take *after* you have invested in an idea and find yourself losing or winning.

For that reason, I have split this book into those two scenarios.

Part I is called 'I'm Losing – What Should I Do?' The chapters in this part deal with being in a situation where you have invested in a great idea and now find yourself losing money.

To help you make the right decisions at such a time I introduce you to the real-life investors who worked for me and examples of their real-life investments.

Throughout the book I have broken down those investors into tribes. I hired them as individuals but as I pored over the data it became clear that there were obvious behavioural groupings among them. They might have operated individually, but their decisions put them into distinct gangs.

In part I we meet three of them: the Rabbits, the Assassins and the Hunters. Each of these groups of elite investors found themselves in many losing situations. Two of the tribes went on to make a lot of money. One of them didn't.

We'll look in detail at the powerful habits of the winners, the Assassins and the Hunters.

We'll also explore the failings of the Rabbits – shortcomings which meant they lost a lot of money and I ultimately had to fire them.

All of us will be able to identify with the Rabbits' weaknesses. The good news is that none of us have to be stuck with them; even they could have changed if they'd identified them and made the choice.

While both the Assassins and Hunters were masters at turning losing situations into winning ones, they adopted vastly different methods to get themselves out of a hole. It is for you to decide which group you feel most at home in.

Part II is called 'I'm Winning – What Should I Do?' and, unsurprisingly, deals with being in the situation of having invested in a great idea and finding yourself sitting on a paper profit.

To help you make the right decisions I show you the mistakes and virtues of the Raiders and the Connoisseurs. Many of you will likely identify with the Raiders, who had a nasty habit of turning winning situations into losing ones. The Connoisseurs, on the other hand, are the role models we should aspire to.

As the tribes describe what investors did in losing and winning positions, some investors belonged to more than one; as you might imagine, a good Assassin could also be an excellent Connoisseur. But a Rabbit was by definition never a Hunter.

For the purposes of anonymity, no individual investor is identified or identifiable by any detail in this book. But all the important information – including the investments – is real and accurate. Every investment described in this book had many millions of pounds, dollars or euros behind it.

When you see big losers and big winners in this book, those losses and wins are real, and one or more of my real-life investors made or lost all that money.

I will demonstrate how legendary investors have been easily led astray by temptations such as a new idea, love or fear – and how the successful ones were able to escape and recover. Anyone who reads this book will be able to use the exact same methods themselves.

Lee Freeman-Shor
London, 2015

"If I have seen so far it is because I have stood
on the shoulders of giants."
– Sir Isaac Newton

PART I

I'm Losing — What Should I Do?

In this part of the book we meet some of the world's greatest investors in losing situations.

These are situations we can all relate to – the investors have lost a lot of money and there is massive uncertainty and negativity surrounding their investments. They are faced with the need to make a crucial decision: to cut their positions or stick with them.

And if they stay invested in a stock, should they invest more money?

Through the Rabbits I will show you the pitfalls you should try to avoid. Through the Assassins and Hunters I will demonstrate exactly what to do if you want a hope of salvaging the situation or indeed turning a loser into a winner.

1. THE RABBITS

Caught in the Capital Impairment

The Rabbits ended up being the least successful investors working for me, but you could never say they weren't prestigious. Many of them were celebrated figures in the City and on Wall Street. One occupied the top floor of a small skyscraper and had meeting rooms with breath-taking views over the City of London through floor-to-ceiling glass windows; a couple of large security guards greeted you before you even got to the marble-floored reception.

Others had decades of experience and name-recognition – some were real 'housewives' favourites'. They were always very likeable and whenever I met them positively oozed success. However, like any investment legend, gaining access to them was easier said than done. For me, you could say it took $50 million. That was roughly the sum each of them ended up managing on behalf of my firm.

As this chapter unfolds you will see why, in the end, I wished I had never met any of them.

JUMPING IN

Let's look at some examples of these investors in action. You'll soon see what was particularly rabbit-like about their investing habits:

CASE STUDY: VYKE COMMUNICATIONS

Vyke Communications was a UK-based company that specialised in software that allowed users to make telephone calls and send text messages over the internet using their mobile phones, computers or normal landlines.

Very big things were expected for this company when one investor started looking at it, not least because it basically meant that users could more or less make international phone calls for free. This seemed like a huge deal. Perhaps Vyke was the next Skype. It could revolutionise global communications.

The investor bought shares in Vyke on 31 October 2007 at £2.10. As it happened, this would be more or less its peak price.

When the stock started to fall shortly after his initial purchase he bought more. So far, so good – this is, after all, what you should do if you are sticking with a stock for the right reasons.

Then it kept falling. The investor chose to stay invested – but he refused to put more money to work.

Roll on two and a half years to 2 July 2010. At that point the investor decided to sell his entire position – with the stock down 99% and trading at £0.02.

Assuming an annual average return for the stock market of 8% per annum, it would have taken this investor 60 years to make all my money back. He needed to produce a return of 9,900% to break even.

CASE STUDY: VOSTOK NAFTA

Vostok Nafta is an investment company listed on the Swedish stock exchange that invests in assets in the Commonwealth of Independent States (CIS), a loose association of some of the countries that used to make up the USSR. Its goal is to coordinate trade and security.

As you might imagine, many of Vostok Nafta's investments have been in oil, gas and mining companies – both private and public. In the past this has led many European investors to purchase its shares as a means of expressing a positive view on commodities; it gave them a leveraged play on that theme.

But more recently Vostok has diversified into consumer-focused companies and has significant investments in Russia's first and only credit card lending company (Tinkoff Credit Systems) as well as an online classified ads company (Avito).

The current Vostok really looks nothing like the old Vostok. It shows just how much things have changed in Russia and its neighbouring countries in the past 20 years. It certainly no longer represents a pure leveraged play on commodities.

On 11 April 2008 an investor bought shares in Vostok Nafta at €9.14.

Five months of unexpected underperformance later and he was persuaded to finally sell at €3.95 – realising a loss of 57%.

It is important to note that the only reason the shares were sold was because I was putting pressure on the investor to either buy more or to sell. The investor did not want to do anything but could not justify why. If I had not intervened, I am pretty sure he would still be holding the stock today.

Assuming the stock reversed course and enjoyed the annual average return for the stock market of 8% per annum, it would take 11 years just to break even.

Phrased differently, having lost 57% of the original capital invested, the reinvested capital would need to produce a return of 133% just to get back to the starting level of capital invested.

CASE STUDY: RAYMARINE

Raymarine is a company that specialises in marine electronics, helping yacht-owners kit out their yachts with radars, satellite TVs, fish finders, GPS gadgets and various other communication devices and bits of equipment.

An investor bought shares in the firm on 31 May 2007 at £4.27 per share.

Roll on 23 months and the stock price had collapsed. The investor was still invested. He was still talking about what a great company it was – though he hadn't yet bought more shares.

One of the reasons the investor put forward for doing nothing was that he was unable to buy more. The stock was too illiquid. Of course, that meant the chilling reverse might also prove true: it might be too illiquid to get out.

In investment circles, this is a schoolboy error. You should never get into something that you cannot get out of in public markets.

The investor also felt that enough money had already been invested.

After pressuring him to do something, he eventually agreed – and managed to sell his entire position on 15 April 2009 at £0.17 per share.

That was a loss of 96% on his original investment. Considering an annual average return for the stock market of 8% per annum, it would take 43 years to break even. He would need to produce a return of 2,463% to get back his original investment.

WHAT THE RABBITS DID WRONG

The Rabbits often dug tunnels that were so deep, they never saw the light of day again. Why did they make this mistake so many times?

"The future may be made up of many factors
but where it truly lies is in the hearts and
minds of men."
– Li Ka Shing

I've used a slightly jokey name for this investing tribe, but the fact is their flaws were very human. I went over all their investments, and it broke down into ten key factors – a range of biases and influences to which every investor is more or less prone, but which the Rabbits failed to control or circumvent through better habits.

By giving in to these factors, they too often ended up caught in the headlights – the results of which were never pretty.

1. Unfashionable insects

One of the most important influences on the Rabbits is what I call **NaFF-Bee** – or *narrative fallacy framing bias*.

I have to admit that every time I think of this term my mind conjures up an image of an insect with poor fashion sense, but it's actually a very important concept.

It is a condition that was alluded to in 1974 by two brilliant Israeli academics, Amos Tversky and his Nobel-Prize-winning collaborator Daniel Kahneman.[3] (Their ideas will crop up throughout these points.)

Tversky and Kahneman suggested that people's decision making is influenced by a cognitive condition they referred to as a *framing bias* or anchoring heuristic. In other words, when people make decisions they tend to reach a conclusion based on the way a problem has been presented.

One of the Rabbits' mistakes was allowing their favourite types of investment to dominate how they looked at a stock. The Rabbit that invested in Vyke loved 'blue-sky' stocks, and because he was looking for shares that might be the big next thing, that's what he saw when a stock gave him half the chance.

NaFF-Bee also goes one step further than this and suggests that we can make up stories to positively explain losing situations.

Look at the following figure. Which company's shares would you buy based on this chart?

FIGURE 1: WHICH COMPANY'S SHARES DO YOU PREFER?

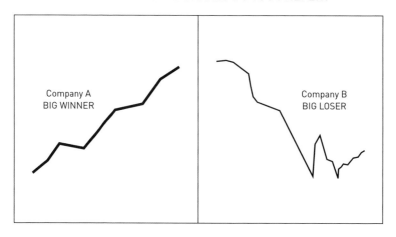

Now look a little more closely:

FIGURE 2: A CLOSER LOOK

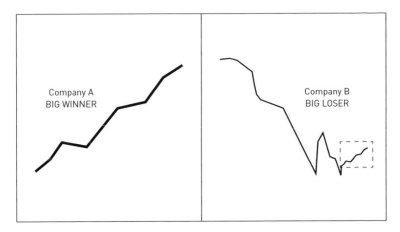

The price charts you see are actually not only for the same stock, they even end at the exact same point. All that's different is the time frame – and how we think about the stock as a result.

One time frame makes you believe the stock is a winner to be snapped up as soon as possible. The other makes you think it is a loser to be shunned.

Both cannot be true at the same time.

Whenever the Rabbits found themselves in a losing position, NaFF-Bee tended to kick in and made them think: "Okay, I have lost money – but my thesis, the story as to why I have invested, is not broken. The share price will turn around and I will still make a lot of money from here."

They were capable of constantly adjusting their mental story and time frame so that the stock always looked attractive.

The Rabbits are a great example of how professional investors often react to a black-swan event – an event they did not anticipate and which has negatively impacted their investment story. They tend to dismiss it. There were problems at Vyke – serious ones, as it turned out. By 2011, the firm was delisted. Soon after, it went bust. The investor was lucky to get out at all.

2. I'm in love

Primacy error was another issue. This describes the way that first impressions have a lasting and disproportional effect on a person.

A classic example of primacy error in real life is love at first sight. It is also demonstrated by newly hatched ducklings. The first living thing they see immediately after hatching they take to be their mother. Thus, if the first thing they see after hatching is you, you will soon have a line of loyal ducklings following you wherever you go.

With the Rabbits, first impressions were often everything. The investor who bought into Vostok had taken a view of the firm some time ago and simply failed to update it to match reality. The net result was that they underreacted when they found themselves losing money.

"Scientists who fall deeply in love with their
hypothesis are proportionately unwilling to
take no as an experimental answer."[4]
– Michael Brooks

I'm afraid that misanthropic investors cannot rejoice at this point (if that idea is not a contradiction in terms): it is perfectly possibly for the opposite of love to be an issue.

Stuart Sutherland in his book *Irrationality* talks about the halo effect and the devil effect. If the first time we are introduced to an investing idea we look at a price chart and see that it has consistently declined for the past ten years, we are likely to classify it as a 'baddy' (a 'dog' as the investment pros would call it). Thereafter this taints our view even when the underlying facts might have changed profoundly for the better. So there can be perfectly good companies shunned for no good reason. Committed value investors will not find this too surprising!

3. Anchor away

A closely related cognitive bias to primacy error is *anchoring* – dropping our intellectual anchor and letting it sink deep into a view and being unwilling to accept new findings that suggest we are wrong and should haul it up and sail the hell out of there.

If a Rabbit did eventually change his mind, it was always an achingly slow process.

It took one Rabbit two and a half years to change his mind on Vyke, and another Rabbit almost two years to react to Raymarine's decline. The other never changed his mind on Vostok. Similar stubbornness occurred on many other investments.

Interestingly, in the investment world, anchoring explains why an earnings surprise typically follows prior surprises. Analysts tend to slowly adjust earnings numbers for a company in their models. No one likes to acknowledge they are wrong, especially if the change requires a complete about-turn. As such, change tends to be a slow process of gradual adjustment. 'Surprise' after 'surprise'.

4. Too soon?

Imagine a scenario where you buy a bar of gold for £1,000. The next day I offer you £500 for that bar. Would you sell it to me? I think most people wouldn't.

Would your response change if I opened the newspaper and showed you that the price of gold had crashed overnight and to sell your bar on the open market would only get you £250?

You probably still wouldn't, and the same would be true of most people. You are anchoring to the £1,000 you paid yesterday. Moreover, you have a vested interest (you own the gold bar), so you believe the bar to be worth more than the price being offered. This is known as *endowment bias*.

If I asked you to name your price for that bar of gold, what would it be? I suspect it would be at least £1,000 given that is your anchor value – the price you paid.

My own experience of managing a team of investors is that large losses that happen over a short duration are almost impossible to accept, especially when they are substantial. It's easier to hold on to a losing position than realise the loss by selling up. Not least because people believe it to be Sod's Law that the price will bounce back post-sale. The Rabbits could not bear the idea of crystallising a loss. They were too aware of how much they had paid for those losing shares.

I want you to now imagine that you have held the gold bar for ten years. Chances are you cannot remember the price you paid for it all those years ago, and I suspect you would be more likely to sell it to me for £500. It would be an easy decision because you would be far less conscious of the anchor value. In addition, I am offering you twice as much as you would receive on the open market so this would appear to be a good deal.

5. The pull of the crowd

I might be singling the Rabbits out for the money they lost me over the years, but the fact is they were rarely unique in the investments they made. Sadly, that was just another reason why they tended to persist with their mistakes.

Neuroscientists have shown that when we don't conform, the amygdala – the part of brain associated with fear – lights up. Going against the crowd makes an investor nervous. Few investors are willing to be a lone voice for fear of others ridiculing them.

And many investors got burnt on the same investments as the Rabbits.

Sadly, this same trait of conforming to peer pressure is why most investors only invest at the end of a bull run. No one wants to be seen as the fool who stood on the side while his neighbours and friends were making vast fortunes.

As a fund manager I can testify that the inner mental pressure to invest in stocks that you do not hold and that are going up is immense. Furthermore, you have to constantly fight the urge to sell stocks that are hurting you. Feelings of pleasure, pain and fear go a long way to explaining investor actions and omissions.

"It is the long-term investor ... who will in practice come in for most criticism ... if in the short run he is unsuccessful, which is very likely, he will not receive much mercy. Worldly wisdom teaches that it is better for reputation to fail conventionally than to succeed unconventionally."[5]

– John Maynard Keynes

---

6. Ego

The Rabbits really didn't like being wrong – they were, in fact, ultimately more interested in being right than making money. Many professional investors I know are, deep down, the same.

Whenever a Rabbit defended a losing investment it reminded me of Warren Buffett's famous saying: "forecasts tell you little about the future but a lot about the forecaster."

The Rabbits all carried false passports – they actually originated from that fictitious country that Nassim Taleb calls Extremistan. They were never going to accept their views were wrong.

The fact is, the greatest minds on the planet can be wrong. My findings suggest you should expect to be wrong at least half of the time. The very best investment minds are!

7. It's not my fault

Behavioural psychologists have a term for when we blame others or external factors for our misfortunes but take full credit when things go well. They call it *self-attribution bias*. It is one of the key reasons we don't learn from past mistakes but keep repeating them.

It never ceased to amaze me how many times the same two villains popped up in the stories told by Rabbits harbouring a losing position: Mr Market ("The market is being stupid") and his sidekick Mr Unlucky ("It wasn't my fault, I was unlucky because of XYZ that no one could have foreseen").

The Rabbits were not only good at blaming these two foes. With Raymarine, one of them was even able to blame illiquidity – a real but entirely optional villain no serious investor should ever encounter – for his inaction.

8. The wrong information

Related to the problems of ego and self-attribution bias, whenever a Rabbit was losing you could always guarantee that he or she would go on a mission to seek out more information to help make the *right* decision.

Unfortunately, undertaking additional research is not as good an idea as it may first appear. For example, if the additional research is carried out by the very same analyst who recommended the stock – as it often is in the City and on Wall Street – naturally his or her focus will be on finding reasons to support the original recommendation. No one wants to admit they were wrong.

Moreover, the analyst will probably be someone the fund manager likes and respects, which means the manager will not be inclined to challenge his or her view.

When you consider all the variables and assumptions that analysts have to deal with before they reach a conclusion, it is mind blowing that they could have any degree of confidence at all.

Because many of the Rabbits had been professionally investing for a couple of decades, controlling a significant amount of assets, they had Rolodexes to die for. When they found the 'story' behind an investment being challenged, they liked nothing better than picking up the phone and dialling the CEO on his or her personal number to get to the bottom of things. Despite being reassured by the CEO that the setback was merely a bump in the road and the media was making a mountain out of a mole hill, the Rabbits would do nothing. They neither bought more shares nor sold their holdings.

A hugely appealing temptation for more information comes from the need to abrogate responsibility in times of crisis. It is very common when a difficult decision has to be made to see the decision-maker involving more people. The more people involved, the more they can relax because if it goes wrong it was not their fault. In companies, the unwillingness of board members to make big decisions that may have far-reaching consequences is the reason financial consultants exist. Boards tend to heavily rely on external advisers when making such decisions.

Various studies focused on betting have shown that while more information increases a person's confidence, it does not increase their accuracy (success ratio).

"Sometimes I have to tell myself to not focus on the math. The danger with the math is that it can make you think you know more than you do. Instead of thinking about what the other player is doing, you end up obsessing over the percentages."[6]

– Johan Lehrer

---

9. Too big to fail

Like many managers, the Rabbits were less inclined to walk away from a large losing investment than a small losing investment. The *denomination effect*[7] described by Himanshu Mishra, Arul Mishra and Dhananjay Nayakankuppam and Priya Raghubir and Joydeep Srivastava[8] helps explain this phenomenon.

Their research showed we find it easier to spend money if we have small denomination coins than when we have larger bank notes. The bigger the losing positions, the more nervous and indecisive most of us become.

This can be more of a problem if you have a smaller portfolio. The investors I worked with readily admitted that in their funds, some of which held up to 100 stocks, it was far easier to sell a losing position because it represented only 1% of the overall fund's net asset value. Thus, if the stock was down 40%, it had only cost them 0.4%. Whereas with the money they managed for me, that stock was perhaps one of only ten positions, each position being on average 10%. As a consequence, to sell meant realising a 4% loss on the total assets managed.

10. I am due a win

Investors like the Rabbits typically suffer from a dose of gambler's fallacy. This is the mistaken belief that the odds for a stock have become *more* attractive due to recent poor performance.

It's the belief that you will win after a streak of losses playing roulette at the casino – "I am due a win."

Even where the odds are 50/50, like the toss of a coin, a deluded gambler believes the odds change in his favour the longer he stays in the game while on a losing streak.

The fact is, the probability of a fair coin turning up heads is always 50%. Each coin flip is an independent event and all previous flips have no effect on future coin tosses.

WHAT THE RABBITS COULD HAVE DONE DIFFERENTLY

The bad news is, everyone can be a Rabbit. The good news is, no one needs to be. There are a few simple things they could have done to overcome their problems.

1. Always have a plan

Investing is all about probabilities. Whether you invest should depend on the odds and the edge you think you have. Given the odds and your edge you should know exactly what you are going to do if the stock you are investing in falls or rises by 20%, 50% and so on.

When faced with a painful loss-making position, most people do nothing. They turn into a Rabbit and procrastinate, letting all their biases play havoc with their decision-making, hoping time will resolve their issues so they don't have to.

The best way round this is to draw up a plan of precisely what actions you will take when your investments don't work. The Rabbits didn't have one. You can.

The necessary actions in a plan are really quite simple. As the next point explains, it all comes down to two choices.

2. Sell or buy more

When you hold a stock that is losing, you feel terrible. You beat yourself up and wish you could turn back the clock. You find yourself unable to sleep.

Some people turn to religion and pray for divine intervention – *"Dear God, if you make the share price go back to the price I paid so that I can get out and not lose money I will be a good investor in the future. I am not asking to make money or be greedy."*

I admit that I have done this on more than one occasion (in the past!). Sadly, it didn't help.

The only solution to a losing situation is to sell out or significantly increase your stake.

You have to ***materially adapt*** if you hope to survive and prosper.

If a stock price is down after your investment, the market is telling you that you were wrong. If you really do believe you were right to invest in that company, then you were clearly wrong in the timing. The sooner you acknowledge you have made a mistake and take steps to deal with it, the better your odds of achieving a successful outcome.

Ask yourself the key question I now ask all of my investors:

"If I had a blank piece of paper and were looking to invest today, would I buy into that stock given what I now know?"

If your answer to the question above is "No", or "Maybe, *but...*" then you should sell.

If you conclude that you would not buy the shares today but find that you cannot push the sell button, be aware that this is because of endowment bias and not a logical investment thesis. Sell.

Legendary investor Peter Lynch adopted a similar approach:

> "[E]very few months I checked the story just as if I were hearing it for the first time ... [and I would] get out of situations where the fundamentals are worse and the price had increased ... and into situations where the fundamentals are better but the price is down ... a price stop is any opportunity to load up on bargains from among your worst performers ... if you can't convince yourself when I'm down 25% I'm a buyer then you'll never make a decent profit in stocks."[9]

Doing nothing when you are losing is *never an option* because if the stock price rises from here you should have put more money to work. If it falls further you should have cut your position.

The Rabbits weren't terrible investors just because they refused to accept they were wrong. The real giveaway was that they refused to do anything when they found themselves in a losing situation.

DATA POINT

LOSERS STAY LOSERS BECAUSE THEY FAIL TO MATERIALLY ADAPT

Out of 941 investments that lost money, when measured from the moment the investor bought the stock to the moment they sold, only 32 (3%) made money thanks to the trading activity of the managers whilst they were invested (by trading activity I mean buying shares in that company after the initial purchase and before the final sale).

It is important to realise that many of these losing investments could have been profitable had the investor *materially adapted* having concluded they were sticking with that investment.

Only a select few investors have the courage to make key changes – even though the benefits of doing so are unmistakeable, as we'll see particularly in chapter 3.

Nowadays, I start to apply pressure on my managers when a stock is down over 20% to ensure action is taken before irreparable damage occurs.

I have learnt that I cannot trust great investors to do the right thing when they are losing – like top athletes, they require coaching and management.

3. Don't go all in

A corollary of the previous point is to never put yourself in a position where you find you are still convinced by your original investment idea but are not able to invest more money when the share price falls. That is poor money management. Keep some powder dry.

This also helps *neutralise* the denomination type of effect – of feeling an investment is too big to be changed.

"In my own portfolios at Pabrai Funds, I adjust for this [getting the odds wrong] by simply placing bets at 10% of assets for each bet. It is suboptimal, but it takes care of the Bet 6 being superior to Bet 2 problem. Many times the bottom three to four bets outperform the ones I felt the best about."[10]
– Mohnish Pabrai

"Action may not always bring happiness, but there is no happiness without action."
– Benjamin Disraeli

---

4. Don't be hasty to jump in, do be hasty to jump out

We should all remember the following wise words:

"It is easier to get into something than to get out of it."[11]

Ned Davis in his book *Being Right or Making Money*, using the Dow Jones Industrial Average from 1929 to 1998, showed that the bulk of investors' losses in bear markets come in the final third of the fall.[12]

This suggests that cutting your losers early is difficult – but makes a lot of sense. Not least because selling out of a stock helps clear your head and enables you to assess a situation more objectively. It's like taking a decongestion pill when suffering from a cold.

And buying slowly over time (known as dollar or pound-cost-averaging), with a reduced position size at the outset, ensures you have plenty of ammunition left to load up when a share finally capitulates (assuming it does).

"[W]hat separates the winners from the losers? The answer is simple – the winners make small mistakes while the losers make big mistakes."[13]

5. Remember there is a difference between 'being right' and 'making money'

Even if you are convinced you are right, remember the saying, *"There is nothing like an idea whose time has come."* In investing, a lot of success can be attributed to being in the right place at the right time – otherwise known as luck.

A classic example of this is Laker Airways, which was founded in 1966 by Sir Freddie Laker. In 1977 this firm introduced the world's first budget airline and operated low-cost flights between London Gatwick Airport and John F. Kennedy Airport in New York.

Due to a combination of recession, high oil prices, changes in currency and simply being ahead of its time, it went bankrupt in 1982. Contrast this with today when there are many airlines successfully operating low-cost, low-frills flights, the most well-known being Ryanair and easyJet in Europe.

6. Seek out opposition

When people lose money they don't want to be told they are wrong. They want reassurance – the same way people sometimes visit a doctor to be told everything is fine.

What you should really do is to speak to someone with an opposing view.

Ideally you should also sell out of the stock while you do that, so that you have removed the emotional attachment of a vested interest. This mitigates endowment bias and you can always buy the stock back later.

If you would not put money to work in a particular share today, knowing what you now know, then you have to concede that the investment is dead – and if you haven't already sold, you absolutely should now.

7. Be humble

As you can imagine, the Rabbits, like many investors, were incredibly smart. Many of them had MBAs, CFAs and other letters after their name that suggested they had an analytical advantage over the rest of the market. The Rabbits were often very confident. And they could be compelling. They never said, "I don't know."

But this is a very dangerous mindset to have. First, it assumes the market is made up of buyers and sellers that are not equally expert, when in fact many will be. Second, 'knowing more' often leads to a person not seeing the wood for the trees.

Throughout history there have been many examples that demonstrate this. My favourites are Harry Warner, of Warner Bros., who in 1927 said, "Who the hell wants to hear actors talk?", and Thomas Watson, chairman of IBM, who in 1943 said, "I think there is a world market for maybe five computers."

Experts are surprisingly bad at forecasting. Falling for your own hype can also often lead to mistakes that the least intelligent person in the world would not be capable of. Warren Buffett, when talking about the collapse of Long-Term Capital Management, marvelled at "10 or 15 guys with an average IQ of maybe 170 getting themselves into a position where they can lose all their money".[14]

And crowds are often surprisingly wise – the market can be right even when everyone who makes it up is individually wrong.

In 1987 Jack Treynor presented 56 of his students with a jar full of jelly beans and asked them a simple question. How many jelly beans were in the jar? There were 850, but not one student got it right – hardly surprising.

What is more surprising is that despite the guesses varying massively from one student to the next, the average number taken from all those wrong numbers was only 2.5% off the actual number of 850. Only one student guessed a number closer to the actual number than the average.

Michael Mauboussin repeated this experiment in 2007 with 73 of his Columbia Business School students and his findings corroborated Treynor's.[15] While the actual number of jelly beans in the jar was 1,116 and the guesses ranged from 250 to 4,100, the average guess from all these 'wrong' guesses was 1,151. That's just 3% off the mark and only two students gave guesses that were closer to the real number of beans than the average of all the wrong guesses.

Remember this the next time you pound the table shouting, "I am right and the market is wrong." My findings show that, on average, only 49% of great ideas make money. If that doesn't scare you then consider this: another study found that fund managers who were 100% confident in picking winning stocks over the next 12 months were right even less – only 12% of the time.[16] You should expect your ideas to be wrong and invest with that in mind.

8. Keep quiet and carry on

Be careful who you talk to about your investments and how you talk about them. Some people have an almost religious zeal for shares they have bought, and like nothing better than sharing their views in public to as many people as possible.

Unfortunately, this makes it impossible to walk away from an idea without looking like an idiot. It's an unnecessary hindrance. The Rabbits might have been less likely to get stuck had they not boasted of anticipated returns.

"Among all forms of mistake, prophecy is the most gratuitous."
– George Eliot, *Middlemarch*

REFLEXIVITY: WHY THE FUTURE IS NEVER CERTAIN

George Soros's reflexivity theory suggests that markets cannot possibly discount the future correctly because they do not merely discount the future; they also help to shape it.

Reflexivity is, in effect, a two-way feedback mechanism in which reality helps shape the participants' thinking and the participants' thinking helps shape reality in an unending process. As such, we should be anything but dogmatic in our views.

9. Don't underestimate the downside – adapt to it

Many of the Rabbits who worked for me loved stocks that could shoot for the moon. They were stocks that had massive potential upside if the story played out. It was no wonder they were keen to jump in.

Unfortunately, unlike financial options, which have a limited loss (the premium paid), these stocks do have a downside – and it can be large. The prospect of huge profits tends to make the possibility of losses dwindle, but that possibility is always very much alive.

The solution is simple: treat them as if they are options. Invest an amount you are willing to lose in the same way that you would pay a one-off lump sum (called a premium) to purchase a stock option. This represents the maximum amount of money you can lose if the option contract closes out of the money.

If the stock does go 'bang' as opposed to 'pop', then the amount you have lost is not fatal.

10. Be open to different kinds of story

Many studies have shown that stocks with the worst stories tend to produce the highest returns.

Stated differently, value investing – investing in cheap stocks that no one likes because they have terrible stories that led to their stock price falling – produce the highest returns over time.

While I am not advocating the avoidance of what I call 'magnet stocks' (or 'glamour stocks'), remember that there are lots of different stories out there.

11. Get sick of sick notes

Over the years I heard many wonderful explanations as to why the Rabbits got things wrong. I always found them amusing.

That said, no one likes admitting they are wrong, especially if we have to report to a boss and explain our actions.

Instead of coming up with increasingly fanciful explanations of why an investment hasn't yet come right, I would urge you to use this tendency to your advantage and do the opposite: familiarise yourself with all the well-worn excuses in advance so that you waste no time trying to fool yourself or anyone else into persisting with a mistake.

Here are some of the excuses I have heard over the years:

a) The 'If only' defence.

b) The 'I would have been right but for' defence.

c) The 'It just hasn't happened yet' defence.

d) The 'Who could have foreseen at the time I invested that XYZ would happen … ' defence.

Peter Lynch in his book *One Up on Wall Street* lists the 12 silliest (and most dangerous) things people say about stock prices. Some of these are well worth including here too:

e) If it's gone down this much already, it can't go much lower.

f) You can always tell when a stock hits rock bottom.

g) Eventually they always come back.

h) When it rebounds slightly, I'll sell.

Having this list of excuses to hand is very beneficial. Check it when you are losing. Are you making any of these excuses to justify not selling?

12. Be suspicious of status

Lastly, whether you work in the investment industry or are thinking about trusting your money to someone who does, there is a bonus moral in the story of the Rabbits: it is dangerous to assume that just because an investment professional is highly educated and has years of experience, he or she will be good at making money and getting the big calls right.

IT'S ALL ABOUT CAPITAL IMPAIRMENT

One of the reasons that the Rabbits held on to losing investments was fear of the unknown: if they sold out, the shares might rally, and they would miss out. It was better to stick with a current loss than worry about that double-whammy.

This is known as *ambiguity aversion*, and describes why people prefer to stick with intolerable situations merely because a hypothetical alternative might be worse. Better the devil you know.

When it comes to losing investments, the facts basically never justify this, and the Rabbits should have used this to fortify themselves against inaction. Here's an example of a Rabbit investment showing how wrong this thinking is:

CASE STUDY: TITAN EUROPE

Titan Europe is an engineering company that designs and manufactures wheels and undercarriage components for off-road vehicles used in the agricultural, construction and mining industries.

It boasts manufacturing and distribution centres in countries as far afield as the USA, Brazil, China and Japan. Its shares went up a staggering 307% after one of my investors sold them on 5 December 2008. This fact alone would be enough to make any investor feel angry, but that is not the point.

In this case, the investor had lost 95% during the previous two years when he held them and the fact is, even if he had chosen to stay invested, he would still have made a loss on the overall investment of 82%.

The only chance to redeem the situation would have been to sell all his other investments and put all the money into the stock when it was down 95%, thus lowering his book price enough to allow him to get his losses back. The problem with that as a strategy is that it is the equivalent of going to the casino and betting everything on black. It either works or it does not. The outcome is binary.

To make money you need to have money. In other words, to maximise profits you *have* to minimise losses. You must preserve your capital. When you are losing you have to materially adapt to mitigate the situation, as you will see when we come to the Assassins and the Hunters. **Permanent impairment of capital destroys wealth.**

DESTROYING WEALTH

My analysis of the 946 investments that lost money (bad buys) revealed that 19 investments, accounting for just 2% of the overall bad buys, lost more than 80%.

131 of those investments (14% of the bad buys) lost more than 40%.

This tells me that the majority of professional investors I worked with appreciated the dangers of losing too much capital.

It doesn't take much to permanently destroy wealth – just being indulgent with one or two losing investments.

When you have lost this much money it takes extraordinarily large returns to make up the lost capital, let alone turn a profit and make money. Here is one final notable example of this in a Rabbit investment:

CASE STUDY: CAPE

I have saved the best case study to last. Make sure you are sitting down and don't have a hot drink in your hand before reading on.

One of my investors bought shares in Cape on 28 September 2007 for £2.79 per share. Cape is considered a global leader in the provision of essential services for the energy and natural resources sectors, ranging from industrial cleaning to painting and coating. It has operations throughout Europe, Africa and Asia.

Unfortunately for this investor, a black swan hit in 2008 in the form of the global financial crisis. This led to cyclical companies with debt on their balance sheets being sold off. Cape, being a company with a small market capitalisation, suffered as investors headed for the doors, and lack of liquidity compounded the problem.

He eventually sold on 10 March 2009 with the share price standing at just £0.18 per share, representing a loss of 94%.

That loss is not the most startling aspect to this story. Nor is the fact that, once it was clear the world would survive the crisis, Cape's share price rebounded and went up an eye watering 1,129%.

The most shocking aspect of this story is that even if he had stayed invested and enjoyed the rebound in the share price, he would still have lost 32%!

Unfortunately, large stock market returns are rare, even if you can hold your nerve and not sell out of one too soon. If you stick with a big loser and do nothing you are virtually guaranteed to be permanently destroying your wealth by creating a hole that is simply too deep to dig your way out of.

I believe that even the best investors often overlook the fact that a stock's price would need a practically supernatural rise of 900% to break even if they have foolishly ridden it down 90% and done nothing. Losing 50% means you need a return of 100% to break even.

Clearly, most of my team knew the danger of suffering big losses and took action before irreparable damage was caused. This is shown by how few large losses we experienced. Overall, we avoided permanently impairing our capital. The remaining chapters show how.

DATA POINT

BYE-BYE BREAKEVEN

For those of you who are curious to know whether the Rabbits recovered their money from staying invested in their big losers, let me satisfy your curiosity. Of 131 investments that fell by more than 40%, only 21 went on to produce returns of over 100%. Odds of ⅙ are not great. And not one produced the required returns to get back to breakeven.

THE LESSONS OF POKER

Stories are the biggest factor in determining what decisions we make. For the Rabbits, the stories in their heads led them to invest many millions in companies that ultimately lost them and me vast amounts of money. Their actions post-investment were clouded by the story that led them to invest on day one.

The moral here is to try to avoid being blinded by your story. Above all, have a **plan of action** as to what you will do if you find yourself in a losing position, even if you still think you are right.

"Nothing proceeded exactly as planned. Yet we managed to construct that docking module anyway."[17]

– Astronaut Col. Chris Hadfield, referring to his first mission where the objective was to construct a docking module on the Russian space station Mir

---

The key difference between the Rabbits and successful investors in this book is that when the Rabbits were losing they did nothing. As we will see with the Assassins and Hunters, they acted decisively to bail themselves out of the holes they found themselves in.

"It is not the strongest of the species that
survive, nor the most intelligent, but the one
most responsive to change."
– Charles Darwin

If only the Rabbits had played poker. Any poker player knows that it is not how many hands you win that matters, it's how much you win when you win, and how much you lose when you lose.

Each hand in poker represents a story and the goal for a poker player is to try to make money with whatever story they have been given – good or bad. If the story is poor then you don't stick with it and throw money at the problem; the odds are stacked against you. You fold your hand, cut your losses and live to fight another day.

Likewise, if you are dealt a good hand but then see the flop and realise the hand is now nowhere near as strong as you thought, you fold.

Billionaire investor Jim Rogers was once quoted as saying "my basic advice is don't lose money".[18] He should know.

2. THE ASSASSINS

The Art of Killing Losses

NEVER LOSE MONEY

Warren Buffett once famously revealed his rules for investing success:

"Rule No. 1 – Never lose money. Rule No.2 – Never forget rule No.1."

The Assassins are the investors who really lived and breathed this principle while working for me. When it came to selling losing positions so as to preserve their capital they were ruthless, like cold-hearted hitmen, pulling the trigger without emotion. Then they carried on with their lives like nothing had happened.

I don't know about you, but whenever I sell out of a losing position I find it very hard to switch off. I relive my mistakes, I castigate myself, I generally feel like the figure in Edvard Munch's painting 'The Scream'.

I also find it very hard to stop checking how a stock is performing after I have sold.

All that misses the point. The point, as the Assassins so clearly understood, is that drawdowns left to their own devices are ultimately what destroys wealth. As we saw in the last chapter, large losses make an overall positive return an almost impossible uphill battle. One should take positive delight in cutting them dead as soon as possible.

If the last chapter didn't persuade you, consider the following table:

TABLE 1: THE IMPACT OF LOSSES

Percentage loss	Gain required to break even
-10%	11%
-20%	25%
-33%	50%
-50%	100%
-75%	300%
-90%	900%

Some notable fund managers take the same approach to losses as the Assassins. Legendary hedge fund manager Stanley Druckenmiller once observed of fellow hedge fund legend, George Soros, that he is

> "the best loss taker I have seen. He doesn't care whether he wins or loses on a trade. If a trade doesn't work, he's confident enough about his ability to win on other trades that he can easily walk away from the position."[19]

The Assassins, like Soros, understood that successful investing is about asymmetric returns. Phrased differently, **winning**

is about ensuring the upside return potential is significantly greater than the downside potential loss.

Despite what you might imagine, in reality we can all be as cold and ruthless as the Assassins.

What I liked about the Assassins was that they lived by a pair of sacred rules.

The rules were derived from their own experience and beliefs, and the key to their success was that when they were losing they would always let the rules, not their emotions or feelings, drive their decisions.

They knew that when faced with the uncertainty that naturally follows when the market has turned against them, they could not rely on themselves to do the right thing.

They therefore committed to becoming slaves to the rules. When a loss occurred they would follow their commandments to the letter.

Importantly, these two rules had been well thought through when the Assassins were in an emotionally 'cold state'. They planned well in advance; before they invested, they knew what they would do afterwards. They did this because they knew that when push came to shove they were likely to make poor decisions in a 'hot' (or emotionally charged) state of mind.

As the old saying from Sun Tzu goes, "battles are won [or lost] before they are fought."

Here are the Assassins' rules for what to do in a losing position, with data from my findings showing exactly why they make sense and example trades showing the Assassins' adherence to them in practice.

THE CODE OF THE ASSASSINS

1. Kill all losers at 20–33%

One of the key secrets of the Assassins was that they knew just how hard it was to actually be a hitman. When it comes time to kill a losing trade, the temptation to wait is overwhelming.

They therefore did not rely on themselves to pull the trigger. Thanks to a simple but sophisticated device, their weapons went off automatically at exactly the right time, taking out their targets without delay.

This device is the humble stop-loss.

The Assassins' rules required them to put a stop-loss in place at the same time that they bought any share. If the stop-loss was triggered by a share price going down a certain amount, it automatically sold their entire stake.

Stop-losses are a common practice in trading but less so in investing (and it is no coincidence that a number of the Assassins were hedge fund managers). Most investors use 'review' prices instead – if one is hit, it forces a review of the holding to decide what to do. In theory this sounds good. The review is designed to wake us up and force us to take action, rather like the alarm on a fridge telling you that you have left the door open. The problem, however, is that too often the fund manager does not shut the fridge door.

Review clauses give the illusion of control rather than actual control. Stop-losses are greatly to be preferred.

So at what level do you set your stop-loss?

Legendary investor and art collector Roy Neuberger, whose investment firm Neuberger Berman bears his name, credits the 10% rule as part of the reason for his success. He always cut his losses when they hit 10% – no matter what.[20] *Recognise your mistakes early and take immediate action* was his mantra.

The Assassins' was the same, but they despatched their losers at slightly different predetermined points depending on their own experience and preferences: almost always somewhere between 20% and 33% (it depended on the Assassin). Despite Neuberger's rule, my findings support the Assassins' approach. This range of stop-loss levels avoids you getting whipsawed while giving a realistic chance of being able to recover from the loss incurred.

A 33% LIMIT

DATA POINT

A loss of 33% requires a 50% subsequent return to break even. My findings show only 11% of the winning stocks (101 in total) that my top investors made produced realised returns of more than 50%. Only 21 of investments analysed realised a return of over 100% – 1% of the investments made

Price targets and a predisposition to snatching profits when winning (see chapter 4) help explain why so few big winners were realised. The reality is, many stocks go up hundreds or thousands of per cent, but few investors stay invested for the duration of the ride. Most sell once they have made a small profit and forsake supernormal returns as a result.

"What makes a system successful is its ability
to recognise losers and kill them quickly."[21]
– James Surowiecki

Here are some examples of the Assassins' stop-loss rule in action:

CASE STUDY: GENMAB

Genmab is a Danish biotechnology company based in Copenhagen that specialises in creating human antibody treatments for people suffering from cancer. At the time of writing, its Ofatumumab product that it is developing with GlaxoSmithKline is in phase three; should it successfully pass this final hurdle it could be a breakthrough for people suffering from leukaemia, non-Hodgkins' lymphoma and rheumatoid arthritis. If it can successfully demonstrate the effectiveness and safety of Ofatumumab then Genmab is sitting on a goldmine.

As it happens, however, this share has not treated investors well in the past. Two weeks after an Assassin put his capital to work in the stock, he found himself sitting on a 30% loss.

His stop-loss activated at -32% and he sold on 16 November 2009 with the shares trading at £12.43, having originally bought into the company on 29 October 2009 when the shares traded at £18.34. As it turns out, his decision to sell was a good one – the shares went on to fall another 49%.

While it was galling to take a 30% loss, he would have found himself down 65% and needing to generate a return of 286% to breakeven. Assuming the average stock market return of 8% per annum, it would take him 14 years to get his money back in nominal terms.

However, because he sold when the stock was down 32% he had the possibility of breaking even in five years using the same assumptions.

CASE STUDY: DODS

Dods is a media company that focuses on providing information, organising events and publishing. All three activities are related to the spheres of politics and the public sector. It is fair to say that Dods has become the most trusted source for political data.

In the UK they provide publications such as Dods Parliamentary Companion *and* Dods Handbook of House of Commons Procedure *to members of parliament and to civil servants tasked with supporting them. In Europe they provide data to members of the European parliament.*

With the library of data they have collected with respect to British parliamentary proceedings going back to 1832, it is hard for any other company to challenge them. They even have their own journalists tasked with covering the latest breaking news and providing high-quality analysis beyond the headlines.

Given this background you would imagine Dods would be a safe investment. What could possibly go wrong?

One Assassin bought shares in Dods on 29 December 2006 when its shares were trading at £0.51. Ten months later, his stop-loss at 39% sold out on 31 October 2007 at £0.31. While a 39% loss was hard to stomach, the stock subsequently fell another 63%. Had he not sold when he did, he would have needed the stock to go up a mind-blowing 435% just to break even – which would take 20 years assuming an average stock market return of 8% per annum.

In the world of investments there is no such thing as a safe bet. If you invest in a company and think that it is bulletproof, I urge you to have an action plan to decide what to do when things go wrong – things often do.

CASE STUDY: ROYAL BANK OF SCOTLAND

It should come as little surprise to find a bank stock amongst these case studies, given all the goings-on in the sector since the 2008 global financial crisis. In the UK, the Royal Bank of Scotland is one of the big banks. Indeed, it is one of three banks, excluding the Bank of England, permitted to issue UK banknotes.

Sadly, nowadays the Royal Bank of Scotland has become synonymous with the credit crunch because it needed to be bailed out by the government, a source of anger for many in the UK. It was deemed too big to fail.

At the time of writing the government owns 82% of the shares outstanding, having been forced to recapitalise the bank in order to prevent a run on the banking system. An Assassin bought shares in the Royal Bank of Scotland on 30 May 2008, before the collapse of Lehman Brothers and the onset of the credit crunch, at £22.29.

As the credit crisis broke, he actually moved quicker than his stop-loss, killing the investment on 3 October 2008 at £18.62, a loss of 16%. The stock then fell a further 82%.

Had he not sold, he would have required his shares in the Royal Bank of Scotland to make a return of 667% just to break even, which equates to 25 years given average market returns. Nursing a 16% loss he can recover that in just two years assuming average market returns.

What amazes me is that investors, unlike traders, rarely use stop-losses. Indeed, many investors frown upon them as crude instruments because they want to have the flexibility to decide what to do instead of mindlessly and mechanically selling.

I believe investors over-look the beauty of stop-losses. They force action at a time when action is required.

DATA POINT

BETTER OFF OUT

Of the 946 losing investments of my top investors, 557 (59%) made money after they were sold. In other words, 41% (389 investments) continued to see their share price fall further.

This might suggest that you should continue to hold onto a loser because roughly six out of ten that were sold subsequently went on to deliver positive returns from the point of sale. However, consider the following: of those 557 stocks, 205 (or 37%) went on to return less than 20%, which may not have been enough for you to recover your losses.

Overall therefore, 594 (389 + 205), or 63% of losing stocks went on to produce a return of less than 20% post-sale, with the majority of those losing money.

As a result, only 352 (946 - 594), or 37% of stocks that had lost the investor money when he sold went on to return more than 20%.

In conclusion, two-thirds of the time you are likely to be better off cutting a losing position.

Part of this is arguably skewed because people tend to sell their winners too soon (something we'll look at later in the book). In other words, the losers could have realised greater returns than 20% had the investor held onto them. Human habits, however, mean riding big winners is very hard to do in practice.

Rumour has it that legendary billionaire investor Paul Tudor Jones II tells everyone:

"Losers average losers, so sell losing positions."

Clearly with good reason.

2. Kill losers after a fixed amount of time

The reasoning behind the Assassins' second rule is best summed up by the old axiom: **Time is money**.

Being in a losing position too long – even if the size of that loss hasn't hit 20% or more – can have a devastating effect on your wealth. This was something the Assassins were acutely aware of.

Why is this the case?

The long-term annual return for stocks, depending on where you take the start and end points, is between 7 and 9% according to most studies. If you earn 9% a year on your investments, this would mean you double your money in eight years.

Let's assume you take out a mortgage and decide to invest a lump sum of money in the stock market to help pay it off. You make the assumption that you will make 9% a year and will therefore be in a position to pay off the mortgage in eight years' time because your initial lump sum will have doubled in value.

Sadly, in the real world, things rarely turn out so smoothly. In this example, you find yourself at the end of the second year with your initial investment down 10%. Not too bad, I hear you say. Only a 10% 'paper' loss – and you still have another six years left before you need the money to pay off the mortgage.

Unfortunately, even a small loss like 10% can have a significant impact. Given you now only have six years left to double your money and pay off your mortgage, you now have to achieve a return of 14.2% per annum to reach your goal – significantly above the long-run average return of the stock market.

Despite these implications you decide to stay invested. You reason that upcoming years in the stock market must give better returns than the long-run average because the previous two years have delivered worse-than-average returns.

Another two years pass, at the end of which you haven't lost any more money, but you haven't gained any either – your investment flatlined and your overall return after four years is -10% in absolute terms (I won't discuss inflation and how the likely real value has fallen by more than this). At this point you figure that you are now 'due' some good fortune and to sell out would be wrong. You reason that you are only down 10%, so it's easy to make up the loss and get back on track to pay off the mortgage in the four years left.

Sadly, you do not appreciate that to be able to pay off your mortgage in four years' time, you now need to achieve a staggering 22.1% per annum return. This is triple the long-term average return of the stock market. Good luck with that.

The Assassins' second rule was therefore to sell stocks which went down by *any* amount and showed no signs of recovery after a certain period of time.

The majority drew the line at six months, but there were variations, as the following data point shows:

DATA POINT

PROFESSIONALS SELL LOSERS QUICKLY

Analysing the figures, 64% (607 bad buys) were sold within six months of initial purchase, whilst 42% (397 bad buys) were sold within three months. Only 17% (157) of bad buys were held for longer than one year.

Indeed, 99% of all bad buys were sold within three years. Stated more starkly, only 12 investments that were realised for a loss were held for longer than three years.

Most professionals sell quickly. I am sure some of that is down to outside pressure from clients or bosses, but even a reluctant Assassin is better than an unrestrained Rabbit.

Large losses kill you quickly, while small losses kill you slowly. The following are some quotes that echo the latter point in particular.

"The best performers force deadlines on themselves."[22]

"Have a time stop ... it is very hard to make up the lost compounding years."[23]

And Jesse Livermore, one of the wealthiest individuals in America at the turn of the 19th century, once said:

"If it feels like a struggle then you should get out."

That sums up exactly the philosophy of the Assassins.

DON'T SELL TOO SOON

It can be very tempting to take assassination to extremes and start cutting losses dead at 5, 10, 15%. Why not despatch the unhappy victims as soon as possible?

It's important to realise that the Assassins' rules did not just protect them from indecision – but from overreaction too.

Below I use real examples from some of my other investors to illustrate what could happen to you if you sell too early (with a loss of less than 20%). These are would-be Assassins, exiled from the gang for over-eagerness. Remember these stock examples are real and had millions of dollars invested in them.

CASE STUDY: COMPASS GROUP

Compass Group is a UK-based business that operates in over 50 countries and is the world's largest food service company (providing contract catering). It serves billions of meals a year for clients including factories, schools, hospitals, universities, major sports venues and offshore oil platforms.

Its Eurest Support Services subsidiary specialises in providing large-scale food services in harsh environments such as conflict zones; the military is a big client.

One of the investors that I managed bought into the group on 30 November 2007 when the shares were trading at £3.19 each. He subsequently sold his entire investment in the company 12 months later on 2 December 2008 with the shares trading at £3.04, incurring a loss of just 5%.

At the time of writing, the stock has gone on to return 143% since it was sold. Sure, the market has rallied and he sold close to the bottom – but the return was more than the market subsequently generated as well.

CASE STUDY: BMW

What is there not to love about a car maker that has captured the imaginations of everyone from corporate fleet managers, who lease 3 Series saloons in staggering numbers, to middle-class mums ferrying their children around in its SUVs? Not to mention middle-aged men who try to recapture their youth driving the executive 6 or 7 Series or the Z4 Roadster ...

One of my investors chose to invest in BMW on 11 April 2008 – just before the credit crunch hit – at a price of €34.95. He sold two months later on 23 June 2008 at a price of €32.35 for a loss of a mere 7%. Before you jump to conclusions, let me assure you that he did not sell because he foresaw the imminent credit crunch. He sold because a better idea had apparently presented itself.

The stock went on to return 95% after he sold it.

CASE STUDY: PIRELLI

Sticking to the motoring theme, we go from German automotive powerhouse to Italian tyre manufacturing behemoth Pirelli. It is the fifth-largest tyre manufacturer in the world, behind Bridgestone, Michelin, Goodyear and Continental. Fans of Formula One will know Pirelli as the sport's current exclusive tyre supplier.

One of my investors bought a stake in Pirelli on 22 January 2010 with the shares trading at €4.61. He subsequently sold just one month later on 9 February at a price of €4.26. A loss of 8%.

As you might expect, I questioned whether my investor had turned into a trader given the brevity of his investment. Pirelli has gone on to return 103% at the time of writing.

CASE STUDY: RIGHTMOVE

In the UK everyone knows Rightmove – it is the default place to search if you are looking for a property to rent or buy. As a result, all estate agents advertise properties on it. This has resulted in Rightmove seeing its turnover increase handsomely year on year. It is basically the Google for British property searches.

One of my investors bought shares in this company when they traded at £5.51 on 13 November 2009. He subsequently sold one month later on 30 December 2009 when the shares were trading at a price of £4.91, a loss of 11%.

The shares shot up 202% following his sale.

WHIPSAWED SORE

Of the 1,866 investments made by my top investors, 421 (22%) were realised for a loss of up to 10%. I discovered that 249 (59%) of these went on to make money. This suggests that if you cut your losses after suffering a minimal loss, you are probably going to be whipsawed.

Moreover, a 10% loss is something that is easily recoverable, even if you have a disposition to take profits when you have made a mere 20%.

BE CAREFUL ON YOUR NEXT INVESTMENT

An Assassins' coldness is a great advantage not only in cutting losing investments dead – it needs to be cultivated in the investment decisions that come afterwards.

Research by Mike Thaler and Eric Johnson suggests that once a person has sold a losing investment, their behaviour turns to risk-seeking, something they coined the "break-even effect".[24] In the presence of prior losses, outcomes offering a chance to break even are especially attractive.

Make sure you don't fall into this trap. I know many professional investors who make this mistake, but this is as much to do with 'career risk' as anything else. They know that if they do not turn their losing situation around they will be fired.

When you sell out of a losing position you are making two decisions:

1. It is no longer a good idea to have the money tied up in that stock.

2. Your money would make a better return invested elsewhere (an opportunity-cost decision).

Only reinvest the proceeds in another stock if that choice is compelling. As Peter Lynch once said:

> "In nine cases out of ten, I sell if company 380 has a better story than company 212, and especially when the latter story begins to sound unlikely."[25]

The approach Lynch is describing is known as the 'pig-in-a-trough approach'. This is where a new idea forces out an existing idea. However, lack of an alternative compelling investment is no excuse for continuing to have money tied up in a low-conviction losing position. Having money sitting in cash gives you an option. Always having your nose in the trough can be very dangerous. As the Wall Street saying goes:

"Bulls win, bears win, but pigs get slaughtered."

AN ELUSIVE CADRE

Selling losers quickly is the key, so why do we struggle to do it?

Perhaps because realising a loss is ten times more painful than living with it merely on paper. Back in 1979, a seminal research paper – again by Kahneman and Tversky – showed that the pain experienced from losing, say $50, was far worse than the joy we experience when we win $50.[26] We find it easy and pleasurable to sell a winning stock, but difficult and painful to sell out of a losing position.

There's also the question of whether a stock might rally after we sell it. The very idea freezes many into inaction.

"In life and business, there are two cardinal sins. The first is to act precipitously without thought and the second is to not act at all."
– Carl Icahn

"There are risks and costs to a program of action. But they are far less than the long-range risks and costs of comfortable inaction."
– John F. Kennedy

The Assassins were some of the most disciplined investors I have met, and a significant factor in their ability to make money was that they cut their losses consistently. A study by Professor Frazzini supports the Assassins' approach too: it shows that the highest investment returns were achieved by those investors that had the highest rate of selling out of losing positions. Those that realised the least amount of losing positions experienced the lowest returns.[27]

The losing trait of riding losing positions while taking profits on winning positions has been called the *disposition effect* by Frazzini. When I hire a new investment manager, I analyse their past trades to see whether or not they unduly suffer from this malady. I only want to work with investors who materially adapt when they are losing.

The way I remember the importance of avoiding big losers is perhaps not very Assassin-esque. I do it with a simple Post-it note. It's stuck to the edge of my computer monitor and it says:

Losers hang around with losers while winners hang around with winners.

I need this reminder because it helps overcome labelling a great investor as terrible because they frequently take small losses. After years of an investor repeatedly telling you that they are wrong, you find yourself thinking, 'This guy is useless, he never gets anything right.' The reality, however, is that they appreciate that the execution of an idea is key, not being right per se. In particular, they know that cutting their losses early matters if they want to be successful.

They are an Assassin. And that is no bad thing.

It took me a few years to appreciate this basic point, and only after I had found that my data empirically supported it did I realise its magnitude for achieving success in investing.

3. THE HUNTERS

Pursuing Losing Shares

In this chapter we meet the Hunters. Like the Assassins, the main reason for their success was what they did when they found themselves in losing situations.

Unlike the Assassins, they did not sell out of those positions – they bought significantly more shares. Rather than killing an underperforming investment and forgetting about it, they stalked their prey – watching it get steadily weaker and lassooing another limb every time it stumbled.

Then they sat back with their prize and waited for it to recover, eventually selling it on for a handsome profit.

In gambling, such behaviour – effectively doubling down – is known as the Martingale approach. It is frowned upon and rightly so: it often leads to ruin.

But in *well-chosen* investments, this is a strategy that wins over time – you acquire more and more assets at cheaper and cheaper prices. When the price of the assets goes up above the average price you have spent, even if it is hardly motoring into new highs, you will be making money.

Let me stress at the outset that the Hunters, like all successful practitioners of what is called 'dollar-cost averaging', planned *beforehand* to buy more shares if a price fell. So they did not go all in on day one. Rather, they invested a lesser amount at the outset and kept some cash on the side – waiting for an opportunity to buy more at a lower price in the future.

The key reason for the Hunters' approach lay in their invariably contrarian style. They were value investors. They generally found themselves buying when everyone else was selling, and this was an extension of that philosophy, another way of exploiting Mr Market when he was acting irrationally.

The approach the Hunters took is a little like the one many of us adopt when it comes to bargains in the January sales – putting off purchases beforehand because we believe what we're after will end up getting sold at a significant discount. Unlike in a January sale, you don't have to queue up outside for hours and fight your way through fellow bargain-hunters: you can slowly acquire more and more of your purchase as its price gets slashed.

SUCCESS STARTS FROM FAILURE

There is a surprising overlap in early investing experiences among the Hunters. Near the start of a significant number of their careers, the Hunters had the good fortune of having a terrible year.

It was a year in which they lost many of their investors a lot of money – and soon found themselves losing a lot of their investors. By the end of one early traumatic period, one Hunter I worked with told me he only had a single client left.

The reason this turned out to be fortunate was because of the lessons the Hunters learned. They are what ultimately led to them delivering returns that made both them and their clients very wealthy indeed.

The Hunters realised that being a contrarian investor is dangerous because you are always going against the crowd. As such they became experts on interpreting charts and other methods to truly gauge the crowd's sentiment. After all, it was no use buying when the crowd showed no signs of changing its mind any time soon.

It burned into their minds the important fact that just because something is cheap does not mean you should buy it.

They also grew unafraid to sell if it became clear they really had made a mistake. Poor value investors I have come across refuse to adapt when they are losing and tend to support their lack of action by saying, "I got it wrong but the stock is simply too cheap to sell now." A bad contrarian investor can make for a very committed Rabbit.

But if a stock still passed the vital 'Would I buy this knowing what I know now?' test, the Hunters followed their plan, and started to put their money on the side to work as the share price dropped.

SNATCHING VICTORY

Some of the Hunters working for me did not simply buy more of a stock if it fell beyond a certain trigger point, say 20%. Rather, they enjoyed trying to pick the bottom, buying in at the greatest possible discount, something that is very hard (if not impossible) to do.

I saw a number of the Hunters get too many of these calls right to think they were playing a losing game. That said, the rest of us are probably better off doing what the others did and simply buying significantly more shares when a stock price falls between 20% and 33% (the reasons for this were covered in the previous chapter: that was the range in which the data made it clear it was sensible to materially adapt).

The exception is if our conviction in a stock has lessened for a good reason. In that case we should do exactly as the Hunters also did, and sell.

I saw the Hunters double or treble their holdings at the bottom on several occasions and then enjoy the rewards as the shares recovered. It was clear that such moments gave the Hunters a real adrenaline kick: apparently there is no better feeling than snatching victory from the jaws of defeat.

Be under no illusions: being a Hunter requires patience and discipline. You have to expect a share price to go against you in the near term and not panic when it does. You have to be prepared to make money from stocks that may never recapture the original price you paid for your first lot of shares. If you know your personality is one which demands instant gratification, this approach is not for you.

"I'm accustomed to hanging around with a stock when the price is going nowhere. Most of the money I make is in the third or fourth year that I've owned something."
– Peter Lynch

Let's look at some examples of the Hunters in action.

CASE STUDY: AKER SOLUTIONS

Aker Solutions is a Norwegian oil services company headquartered in Oslo. It is a global provider of products and services related to the construction, maintenance and operation of oil and gas fields.

One of my Hunters bought this stock on 14 April 2008 at an initial price of €15.84 per share. Roll on a year and a half and the share price had plummeted. On 28 September 2009 my investor seized the opportunity to exploit Mr Market and bought significantly more stock so as to reduce the average price paid for his overall position to just €7.61.

On 28 January 2010 he sold his entire stake in the company with the shares trading at €9.58 after recognising his original thesis was no longer valid. Had he not done anything he would have realised a loss of 40%. However, by having the courage of his convictions to buy significantly more shares when they were depressed, he sold out of the position having made a profit of 24%. The Hunter turned a loser into a winner.

CASE STUDY: EXPERIAN

Experian is an Irish company with operations all over the globe, including the USA. The company collects information on individuals and produces credit scores which are used by lenders to decide whether to extend credit to applicants or whether to give them a loan such as a mortgage. If you have ever been turned down for a loan following a credit check, chances are that the report the loan officer used to make his or her decision was generated by Experian.

This paints a picture of a rather bulletproof business model because so many companies rely on Experian's reports in the day-to-day running of their businesses. What could possibly go wrong?

A Hunter bought the stock on 13 June 2006, at an initial price of £9.02 per share. Despite holding out through the credit crunch, this Hunter subsequently sold his entire stake five years later on 1 September 2011 with the shares trading at £7.06 per share. Had he done nothing, his patience as a buy-and-hold investor would not have been rewarded and he would have realised a loss of 22%. So much for the saying, 'Time is your friend when losing'.

Fortunately, the Hunter had bought more shares in the company when they fell in price during that period. This reduced the average book price of his shares to £5.66 per share and meant that when he did sell he realised a profit of 19% and not a loss of 22%. Whilst 19% does not represent an earth-shattering investment, and you could argue that he should have sold and deployed his capital elsewhere, it is clear that the investor added significant value through his actions. He turned a loser into a winner. This is the type of investor I want on my team.

CASE STUDY: TECHNIP

Technip is a French project-management, engineering and construction firm for the oil and gas industry. It is seen as a world leader in what it does – whether subsea drilling, laying specially built pipelines, producing floating offshore platforms or helping to plan the development of an oil or gas field.

One Hunter bought this stock on 11 April 2008 at an initial price of €55.42 per share, and sold it just over two years later on 21 May 2010 when the shares were trading at €52.13 per share.

On the face of it, this was a poor investment that lost 6% and tied up capital that could have been better deployed elsewhere. However, this Hunter stuck to his process of buying materially more shares in the company if the share price falls and nothing otherwise has changed. He bought heavily during the two-year period when the shares sold off.

By doing this he managed to reduce his average book price per share to €42.24. This meant that instead of realising a small loss he actually realised a gain of 22%.

CASE STUDY: THOMSON REUTERS

Thomson Reuters is a multinational media company based in New York. It is one of a number of leaders at providing the very latest content and data to the finance industry. It produces material to help lawyers and accountants ensure they are meeting their requirements of continued professional education. It also produces research for the pharmaceutical industry. On the face of it, this looks like a solid business with attractive end clients. Surely nothing could go wrong?

A Hunter bought the stock on 13 June 2006 when the shares were trading at £22.25 each. Three years later he decided to sell his entire stake in the company, with the shares trading at £18.92 per share on 10 September 2009.

Thankfully, because he had bought materially more shares in the first few years of his holding when the share price had fallen, he was able to reduce his average book price to £15.82 per share. This meant that instead of realising a loss of 15%, he made a profit of 17%.

HUNTING FOR THE COMPOUNDING EFFECT

Apart from discovering that $E=MC^2$, Einstein was also famous for saying:

"Compound interest is the most powerful force in the universe."

John Larry Kelly Jr, a famed mathematician, showed that the way to create wealth was to invest in a manner that attempted to maximise the geometric mean of returns. By doing this you would exploit the power of compounding and become rich in the shortest possible time.

I do not intend to go into the detail of the Kelly Criterion as it is now famously called, but suffice to say this formula shows that you should invest big when the odds are great and you have an edge.

Warren Buffett is the most famous exponent of this approach. He invested 42% of Berkshire Hathaway in American Express in 1974 because he thought the odds were outrageously in his favour and he had an edge in his assessment of how that business would perform in the decades ahead.

One of the reasons that being a Hunter works so well is that it provides you with such opportunities.

If a stock you are invested in has fallen materially in price, but nothing else has changed – the investment thesis is still in tact – your odds will have improved significantly and you should materially increase your stake in that company.

One of the Hunters invested 20% of the assets he managed on my behalf in Barclays shares when they traded at just 55p in 2009, having been battered during the global financial crisis in 2008. The shares rebounded and he made a lot of money.

The key point here is that although the Hunter invested big in Barclays at the outset, he was prepared to invest a lot more money should it continue to fall, because the odds would have gone from great to extraordinary.

If you believe the way to control risk is to have a diversified portfolio, then obviously you have no choice but to invest small stakes in each company.

If you are a Hunter, though, you choose not to control risk by diversification but by thoroughly understanding the risk and returns of a particular stock or handful of stocks. Your goal is to find companies that have an unbelievably attractive, asymmetric payoff profile.

The fact that you are only investing in a few companies means that you have the opportunity to invest big on day one, and then follow up with large top-up investments should the share price fall. As Warren Buffett said in his annual letter to the shareholders of Berkshire Hathaway in 1993:

> "If you are a know-something investor, able to understand business economics and to find five to ten sensibly-priced companies that possess important long-term competitive advantages, conventional diversification makes no sense for you. It is apt simply to hurt your results and increase your risk. I cannot understand why an investor of that sort elects to put money into a business that is his 20th favourite rather than simply adding that money to his top choices – the businesses he understands best and that present the least risk, along with the greatest profit

potential. In the words of the prophet Mae West: *Too much of a good thing can be wonderful.*"[28]

The Hunters often put 20% of their assets in a single stock, and had to be comfortable investing another 20% in that same stock when it was heading south.

Most of us would suffer sleepless nights knowing that we had invested 40% of our money in a single stock. One way of dealing with this is obvious. Choose to only review the position every five years or set up an alert on your trading account to inform you if the price drops by a certain threshold. It never ceases to amaze me how being ignorant of share price swings helps a person stay invested in a large position.

I would also advocate setting up standing orders in the market when you buy your first stake in a company. It is very easy to freeze with fear when shares drop – even if it's to a price that we said at the outset we would be happy to buy more shares at.

Mohnish Prabai talks about having a crystal-clear exit plan before you ever think about buying a stock.[29] I agree – but also advocate having a clear plan for topping up losers as well.

THE ADVANTAGES OF A HUNTER

In the tables below I show the hypothetical investment activities of a Hunter, an Assassin and a Rabbit, so that you can appreciate the power of the Hunter's approach. All start out with $900 to invest.

The Hunter adopts the three-bites-at-the-cherry approach to investing, which means that he initially invests a third of the total amount he is willing to invest in the stock. If the price falls beyond a certain threshold, he invests another third. If the price falls yet further, he will deploy his final third of remaining capital in the stock.

The Rabbit invests his entire stake, $900, in one go and adopts a buy-and-hold approach. The Assassin also invests his entire stake of $900 in one go but will only keep holding it if it doesn't hit the stop-loss set at 25% below his original purchase price.

Here is an overview of each strategy over the next four years:

RABBIT'S P&L

Year	Share price	Shares bought	Shares sold	Total book cost	Average price paid	Profit or loss
2011	$100	9	0	$900	$100	$0
2012	$75	0	0	$900	$100	-$225
2013	$50	0	0	$900	$100	-$450
2014	$90	0	0	$900	$100	-$90
Overall profit or loss						**-$90**

ASSASSIN'S P&L

Year	Share price	Shares bought	Shares sold	Total book cost	Average price paid	Profit or loss
2011	$100	9	0	$900	$100	$0
2012	$75	0	9	$900	$100	-$225
2013	$50	0	0	$900	$100	-$225?
2014	$90	0	0	$900	$100	-$225?
Overall profit or loss						**-$225?**

HUNTER'S P&L

Year	Share price	Shares bought	Shares sold	Total book cost	Average price paid	Profit or loss
2011	$100	3	0	$300	$100	$0
2012	$75	4	0	$600	$86	-$75
2013	$50	6	0	$900	$69	-$250
2014	$90	0	0	$900	$69	+$270
Overall profit or loss						**+$270**

As can be seen, after four years of investing in a disciplined pound-cost-averaging fashion, the Hunter has made $270 profit.[30] Being willing to stick with the losing position and buy significantly more shares paid off.

The Rabbit, on the other hand – who, like the Hunter, also stayed invested throughout – is showing a loss of $90 because he went all-in on day one and subsequently did nothing. By going all-in, the Rabbit lost the 'optionality' to buy more shares when they fell in price – his fate was tied to that one point and one price.

On the face of it, the Assassin did the worst. He lost $225 and sold out. However, whether he was the worst investor depends on the returns he experienced from deploying the remaining $675 in other investments over the next two years.

Three choices, but only two make sense

As you can see, if you find yourself invested in a stock that is losing money, you have to decide whether to be an Assassin (cut and invest the proceeds elsewhere) or a Hunter (invest more money in that stock). I do not propose to tell you which approach to adopt. You will know yourself which approach best suits you.

A RARE INVESTING STYLE

My experience of managing an elite group of professional investors is that when the shares of a high-conviction company fell in price, most invariably stayed optimistic (rightly or wrongly). Most gave me chapter and verse as to why the story and the fundamentals had not changed, and why it still remained a great investment idea. *But most did not buy materially more shares.*

This was madness. If they were telling me it is still a wonderful company and the millions of pounds they had lost would be recovered, why would they not buy materially more shares when this amazing company's shares were now trading significantly below the price at which they first bought them?

One powerful technique I found useful in persuading some of the investors to add to a losing position was to get them to look beyond their current position and at their broader portfolio. If the overall portfolio was making money I could say to them, "Look, you are in profit and can afford to add to the losing position – why not put some of that profit to work?" Or, if they were sitting on cash, I would point out that the return expectations of the battered stock had to be better than the return offered by cash. Especially in a zero-interest-rate world.

I am sure the professional investors who worked for me were not unique in their reluctance to adopt the approach of the

Hunters. The reasons underlying their reticence to deploy more capital in a losing stock were varied.

1. Outflows – Most funds are priced daily and clients can invest or disinvest in a fund on a daily basis. If you are managing a fund suffering from redemptions, not only are you unable to buy a stock that has been beaten down, you might actually have to sell to meet the redemptions, further compounding the problem.

2. Not enough cash or no inflows – I experienced this problem with one of the managers I used to manage. He did nothing when his shares got beaten up unless he was fortunate enough to get an inflow of cash at that time. He did not keep any cash on the side to give him the option to top up a loser, nor did he take some profits from other positions to top up the losing ones. Most fund managers I have met seem to have an aversion to selling down or selling out of another stock to invest more money in a losing one. Deep down they likely fear they will compound their initial mistake.

3. Peer pressure – The pressure felt by professional money managers when things are not working in the short term can be intense. Often it will lead them to make the wrong decision – they do nothing because they rationalise that they are damned if they do and damned if they don't.

The effects of peer pressure in the investment industry were strikingly exemplified in an article about a court case brought by a fund manager, Patrick Evershed, against his former employer, the ill-fated asset management firm New Star:

"Evershed's account of life at New Star has revealed a culture of fear, with allegations that bullying and the humiliation of staff was commonplace. It includes John Duffield, New Star's founder, withdrawing an offer of sweets from managers having a bad period of performance, as well as accounts of him pacing around the office calling managers names. Evershed said he believed the 'much publicised demise of New Star was as a direct result of Duffield's bullying, his interference with the way in which the fund managers managed their funds and his refusal to take on board anyone's advice. He (Duffield) would prowl around the floor on a regular basis with his jaw jutting out and emitting growling sounds and call us "morons" and "criminals". He knew how every fund was performing each hour and he would compare our performance against each other in such a way as to cause distress to those who had had a bad hour or day', Evershed claimed. New Star's formal response to his grievances – made via letter in 2009 – saw Duffield admit to offering sweets to managers but deny ever withdrawing them based on fund performance. Evershed described the atmosphere at work as horrendous and extremely unpleasant, stating it was 'so intimidating, so humiliating, so distressing'."[31]

As Michael Lewis put it in *Moneyball*, most failing strategies fail because they all have one thing in common; they are designed with fear of public humiliation in mind:

> "Every change he made was aimed more at preventing embarrassment than at achieving success. To reduce his strikeouts he shortened his swing, and traded the possibility of hitting a home run for a greater likelihood of simply putting the ball in play."

> "Managers tend to pick a strategy that is least likely to fail … the pain of looking bad is worse than the gain of making the best move."

No one is immune to this. Research in the 1950s by American psychologist Solomon Asch showed just how susceptible we all are. If several people around you are shown the colour red and are then asked what colour they see, if they all say "green", then most likely you will also say "green". No one is ever trading in isolation – whether in the City or on Wall Street, or at home in our pyjamas, we are part of a larger community that tends to move as a herd. Peer pressure has the ability to prevent us taking the right decision to either buy more shares or sell out.

4. Prior price movement – The price movement of the stock prior to your purchase matters because of representative bias, a term again first coined by Tversky and Kahneman.[32] Quite simply, a stock price that has gone up is seen as 'good' and will attract buyers, while a stock price that has gone down is seen as a 'dog' and will be shunned by all but the bravest investors. As such, most will choose to stand on the side and wait for the stock they hold, and which has lost them money, to recover rather than getting involved while the price is still falling (this is known as the bystander effect[33]). Adding to a loser is seen as a 'bad' idea, but so, perversely, is selling a loser.

Remember, losers hang around with losers and do nothing to get themselves out of their position.

CONCLUSION TO PART I

In the first part of this book I have attempted to show that success often arises from what you do when you are losing. My findings reveal that you can get big decisions wrong and still make money provided you are willing to materially adapt.

Below I have put together a decision matrix showing the consequences of the Rabbits', Assassins' and Hunters' decisions. This matrix clearly shows that doing nothing is never an option.

DECISION MATRIX			
Who/action taken	Stock price goes up	Stock price goes down	Stock price stays same
Rabbits do nothing	Wrong	Wrong	Wrong
Assassins sell	Possibly wrong	Right	Right
Hunters buy	Right	Possibly wrong	Possibly wrong

In my management of investment talent I focus relentlessly on what my investors do when they are losing. You cannot change the past but you can change the future.

Many professional investors neglect to focus on the execution of the idea. Proof of this can be seen in the way a typical investment house is set up. They will typically have hundreds of highly educated analysts whose job it is to come up with stock ideas, from which a fund manager cherry picks the best ones for his or her portfolio. Furthermore, when the fund manager puts together this portfolio of stocks, he or she is focused on how these stocks correlate with one another to manage risk as opposed to how he or she will execute each of the ideas.

A more forward-thinking approach would see resources just as much – if not *more* – focused on helping the fund manager execute the investments well. I find it bizarre that top athletes and sportsmen and women have coaches but the majority of investment professionals do not.

How can they expect to improve their game if they do not have constructive feedback?

PART II

I'm Winning — What Should I Do?

In Part I, I introduced you to three different investing tribes – the Rabbits, the Assassins and the Hunters – and demonstrated how good execution of a losing idea can not only salvage a losing position but turn it into a winning one.

In Part II we will meet two further gangs of investors, the Raiders and the Connoisseurs. Through them I will endeavour to show you what you should and should not do if you find yourself in the fortunate position of holding a winning stock.

You might think that being in a winning position makes things a lot easier, but it pains me the number of times I have seen professional investors destroy wealth by doing the wrong thing when they are winning. Many are 'anti-alchemists', turning gold into lead. Worse still, they get paid a lot of money for doing it.

As in Part I, the villains and heroes you meet on the following pages are a number of real, very famous investors, and all the trades you see are real too.

4. THE RAIDERS

Snatching at Treasure

Raiders occupy a thin line between success and disaster. These are investors who like nothing better than taking a profit as soon as practical. They are the stock market equivalent of golden-age adventurers: having penetrated through the dense jungle, found the lost temple or buried treasure, they fill their pockets with all the ancient coins and gems they can – then turn tail and run.

Unlike golden-age adventurers, they are rarely chased by angry locals or rivals. The only boulders rolling after them are in their imaginations. They are terrified of getting caught and losing everything, and to ensure they at least come away with something end up leaving countless chests and swag-bags of treasure behind completely unnecessarily.

It's a sad case of what you might call premature evacuation.

I was lucky to have some successful Raiders investing for me who more often than not *did* find treasure – so it added up to profit in the end (even if it wasn't as much as I would have liked). But it would only have taken getting caught in one or two well-primed temple traps to end their adventures for good.

And not all of the Raiders were so lucky – even one with an incredible record of good calls came a cropper in the end.

This chapter, therefore, is cautionary. When winning, you do not want to do what the Raiders did.

INVESTING ON THE EDGE OF RUIN

I discovered the Raiders when I noticed the rather distressing fact that one of my investors had an incredible success rate – almost 70% of his ideas were correct, which is truly phenomenal – but he hadn't made me any money.

I broke down the data for his investments and discovered that whenever he made a small gain, say 10%, he would immediately sell the stock and take the profit.

Interestingly, he was a hedge fund manager and in his own trading was an expert at shorting shares – and staying short. But when it came to long-only investments, he and the other Raiders lacked a key habit that the successful investors I worked with possessed. He did not embrace the right tail of the distribution curve. In ordinary terms, the Raiders did not run their winners.

Let's look at some unhappy examples of this in action:

CASE STUDY: CHICAGO BRIDGE & IRON

Chicago Bridge & Iron (or CBI) is a large multinational company that likes to think of itself as a one-stop shop for energy industry infrastructure projects.

One of the Raiders bought into CBI on 3 September 2009 when the shares were trading at the sterling equivalent of £10.66. One month later, on 5 October 2009, he sold with the stock trading at £12.29 per share.

I spoke to the investor about this and it was clear he felt very pleased with himself, bagging a tidy profit of 15% in just one month. But, as I write, the stock is trading at the sterling equivalent of £30.38 per share. In other words, the stock went up another 147% post-sale.

The investor in question did not reinvest the proceeds of his sale into another idea that produced anything near as high a return as this.

Assuming an annual average return for the stock market of 8% per annum, this Raider voluntarily gave up 12 years' worth of returns by bagging his profits too early.

CASE STUDY: BRITISH AMERICAN TOBACCO

British American Tobacco, as the name implies, manufactures and sells tobacco products. While you may not have heard of the firm itself, you may be familiar with some of its famous cigarette brands. These include Lucky Strike, which is particularly popular in the USA, and Pall Mall, the third biggest cigarette brand in the world. Other brands include Vogue, John Player, Benson & Hedges and Kent.

One of the Raiders I managed took the view that the cigarette giant had seen the bottom in its share price on 3 July 2009, so he bought the stock when it was trading at £19.96 per share. Two and a half months later, on 21 September 2009, he sold at £21.75 per share, making a profit of 9%.

I don't mind telling you that when I met this investor, he was very smug, having bottom-picked the market. Unfortunately, I was less than amused. I thought I had hired an investor, not a trader.

After he sold the stock it continued to go up. At the time of writing it trades at £37.93 per share – a further 74%. Assuming an annual average return for the stock market of 8% per annum, this Raider voluntarily gave up seven years' worth of returns.

CASE STUDY: SWEDISH MATCH

Sticking with the tobacco theme, one of the Raiders I managed also invested in Swedish Match. This company is a world leader in chewable tobacco (not matches). This investor bought into the stock on 10 October 2008 when the shares were trading at the equivalent of €10.56 per share.

This investor stayed invested for just two months, selling at the equivalent of €10.18 per share on 16 December 2008 at the height of the global financial crisis, thus suffering a small loss of 4%. He then decided to buy back into the stock on 24 June 2009 at €11.23 per share, before selling out of the stock again on 22 April 2010 with the stock trading at €17.54 per share. Second time around, he made a profit of 56%.

I imagine many of you are thinking, "What is wrong with that?"

Well, had he stayed invested he would have made 145% (at the time of writing the stock is trading at the equivalent of €25.88 per share – a further increase of 49% since he sold the second time around).

CASE STUDY: NOVO NORDISK

Novo Nordisk is a Danish pharmaceutical company that is the world leader in diabetes medications (insulin) and care equipment (injection devices and needles). It also has a leading position with respect to haemophilia care and hormone-replacement therapy.

One of the investors I managed chose to invest in Novo after the stock had been doing nothing much for a while. He initiated a position on 22 April 2009 at the equivalent of €35.71. He later sold the stock on 4 December 2009 when it was trading at €45.32 per share, making a decent profit of 27%. I can picture him running around his office giving his co-workers big high fives.

Unfortunately, after he sold, the stock continued to go up. As I write, it is trading at €124.92 per share, a further increase of 175%. Assuming an annual average return for the stock market of 8% per annum, this investor voluntarily gave up 13 years' worth of returns.

Time and time again my analysis showed that had the Raiders stayed invested in their winning ideas, they would have gone on to make a lot more money.

Furthermore, because of this failure to run their winners, a few large losses in due course wiped out most of the Raiders' small gains. The Raiders were a good example of investors that are right most of the time and still lose money. They have high hit success rates but poor payoff profiles.

THE DANGER OF CUTTING YOUR WINNERS

Reviewing all the trades that my investors made, I wanted to see on average how detrimental it was for a manager to take a profit when the stock was up by 20% or less.

In total, 611 stocks (66% of all winning investments) were sold for a profit of less than 20%. Of these, 370 (or *61%*) kept going up and, had the investor stuck with them, he or she would have made even more money.

While the magnitude of subsequent outperformance differed, the fact is that big winners were to be found amongst those 370 names.

Moreover, the most successful investors I worked with, those that made the most money, all had one thing in common: the presence of a couple of big winners in their portfolios. Any approach that does not embrace the possibility of winning big is doomed.

I think we can all relate to the Raiders' desire to take profits on winning investments. The problem is that taking small profits is like picking up pennies in front of an oncoming train. It only works until the train comes along.

WHY DO INVESTORS SELL TOO SOON?

There are a number of key reasons that these investors became Raiders. Looking back on my time with them, the following stand out as reasons that they repeatedly sold too soon:

1. It feels so good

Selling for a profit is a nice feeling. When we win, testosterone and dopamine are produced and these hormones make us feel good. So damn good that we want to do it again – and again and again.

As any smoker will tell you, it is hard to stop doing something that gives you pleasure.

The Raiders were effectively drug addicts. They weren't constantly snorting lines of cocaine with rolled up snippets of the *FT* – but they had become addicted to the chemicals their bodies would release whenever they took a profit.

2. I'm bored

Reflecting on selling his investment in Warner Bros, legendary investor Peter Lynch admitted, "I got bored."[34]

Getting tired of waiting for action is part of human nature. Lynch summarised the problem well: "it's normally harder to stick with a winning stock ... than it is to believe in it after the price goes down."[35]

3. Frustration

Nothing is truer than the saying, 'feel the pain of the gain' when it comes to staying invested in a winning position.

Staying invested in a winning position is like taking the kids on a day out to the zoo but you have a two-hour car drive before you get there. Halfway through the journey they start asking, "Are we nearly there yet?" in ever louder voices. Three quarters of the way there, they begin kicking the seats.

The only way to get to the zoo and ultimately enjoy your day is to put up with the pressure and not give in.

SELF-CONTROL ISSUES

These first three issues tend to go together: we have self-control problems when faced with a decision today that is very pleasurable, like taking profits. We find it very hard to say, "No." Various studies have shown that humans prefer $1 today versus $2 tomorrow, a phenomenon that has been termed hyperbolic discounting.[36]

Raiders are 'present-biased' without realising it.

"In the morning, when temptation is remote, we vow to go to bed early, stick to our diet, and not to have too much to drink. That night we

stay out until 3:00am, have two helpings of chocolate decadence, and a variety of Aquavit at a Norwegian restaurant."[37]

4. Fear

The research of Shlomo Benartzi and Richard Thaler also showed that the pain of a short-term loss overpowers the pleasure of a long-term gain. This myopic (short-term) focus and a hatred of losing they called *myopic loss aversion*.[38]

This produces a fear which turns many investors into Raiders when a share starts doing well.

The findings of Terrance Odean suggest that this problem has grown thanks to the unprecedented immediacy of the internet. He discovered that people who traded via telephone from 1991 to 1996 outperformed the market by 2.4% per year on average. However, when they changed to trading online they underperformed the market by 3.5% per year.[39]

Incidentally, Odean also found that stocks investors switch into after selling winners tend to underperform the old ones by 2.3%.[40] Investors think they are getting rid of weak winners and replacing them with stronger ones, but in fact they are usually doing the opposite.

5. Short-termism

Many an investor becomes a Raider because of a natural disposition to focus on the short term. The technical term for this is *recency bias*.

My own fund – the Old Mutual European Best Ideas fund – is a good example of this in action. If you took a three-year view from 2009 to 2011 you would have said I was a superstar. If you viewed my performance during August 2011, or for the year 2011 alone, you would have said quite the reverse.

The flows my fund experienced showed just this. Shortly after delivering those three-year performance figures I had over $200 million invested into my fund. But during August 2011, clients withdrew tens of millions of dollars.

Since 2011 the performance of the fund has been strong and, surprise surprise, we have attracted inflows again.

Imposing different time frames on an investment can produce very different results – and Raiders invariably impose short-term ones. This can be deadly for winning trades. Many investors seem to have a dangerous habit of buying high (a prior big winner) and selling after a small gain. They like to strike while the iron is hot.

6. Risk aversion

In 1979, Tversky and Kahneman published another ground-breaking paper introducing what they called *prospect theory*.[41] The paper dealt with how people make choices in the face of uncertainty and risk. Kahneman and Tversky found that whether a person is winning or losing affects how they make a decision. People are risk-averse when winning, hence they take profits – but risk-seeking when losing.

It seems the driver behind this human habit to take profits early is related to the 'certainty' of the outcome an individual is facing, and whether that outcome is desirable:

• When losing, risk is appealing because anything is better than a certain loss.

• When winning, selling is appealing because the certainty of a small victory is better than the uncertainty of a loss or greater victory.

THE SECRETS OF THE BOXES

Many readers will be familiar with the TV show Deal or No Deal. *The concept is very simple. There are 26 boxes and hidden in each is a cash prize between one pence and one million pounds. One by one the contestant has to discard a box and forfeit whatever prize money is inside it.*

At various points in the game the contestant will be offered a cash prize by a 'banker' to walk away and thus forfeit whatever prizes are left in the remaining boxes.

The bigger the potential prize left in the remaining boxes, the keener the banker is to try to get the contestant to accept the alternative cash prize.

Thus, you could have two boxes left, one with £1m inside and the other with £50,000. The banker might offer you £150,000 to walk away.

Many people do take the certain £150,000 instead of risking walking away with 'just' £50,000.

It's emotionally very hard to risk losing a certain profit for a potentially bigger, but uncertain, profit, and most cannot do it. The behavioural economics experts Dan Ariely and Ziv Carmon undertook a fascinating study of Deal or No Deal *which every investor who feels the temptation to be a Raider should read.*[42]

"We have an irrational tendency to be less willing to gamble with profits than with losses. This means selling quickly when we earn profits but not selling if we are running losses."[43]

– Lars Tvede

WHY YOU SHOULDN'T SELL EARLY

If the example investments earlier weren't enough to persuade you of the folly of being a stock market Raider, here are five big reasons that it makes no sense.

1. Rarity value

Big winners are rare and I am yet to see a successful investor who has not 'hung around' with big winners.

All the successful investors I have managed made money because they won big in a few names, while ensuring the bad ideas did not materially hurt them.

Having a process that prevents you winning big because you take profits once a stock is up 20 or 30% means that you could potentially be the person who gives away a winning lottery ticket.

And not all profits are equal. In the long term, investing in stocks is one of the best ways to make money – but while this is true as a whole, if you are buying individual shares it very much depends on the stocks you buy. Stock market returns over time show *kurtosis*, which means fat tails are larger than would be expected from a normal distribution curve.[44] This means that a few big winners and losers distort the overall market return – and an investor's return. If you are not invested in those big winners your returns are drastically reduced.[45]

"Extremes dominate our world and we think
they are the norm."[46]
– Terry Burnham and Jay Phelan

RABBITS AND RAIDERS

*Raiders are often Rabbits when they're losing – and the combination
is fatal.*

*If you combine the urge to sell winners too soon with the reluctance to
sell losers, the net result is losing a lot more than you win: you have
effectively got an investment style that combines significant downside
risk with insignificant upside potential.*

*As Peter Lynch put it: "Some people automatically sell the winners
and hold on to their losers … which is about as sensible as pulling
out the flowers and watering the weeds."[47]*

FIGURE 3: WHAT A LOSING INVESTMENT APPROACH LOOKS LIKE

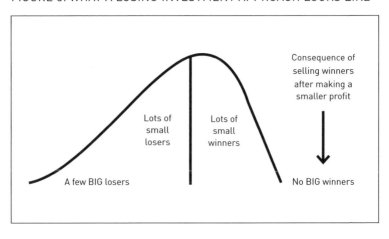

Taking small profits means you never win **BIG**.

2. Beat your rivals

The bad news about being a Raider, as we have seen, is that it is so incredibly tempting for most people.

But that's also good news: it means that honing the ability to run winners can give you a very easy but significant advantage over your rivals.

 PREMATURE PROFESSIONALS

Of the 1,866 investments that I analysed, only 21 (or 1% of all investments) returned more than 100%.

My findings show that 42% of profit-taking by many of the world's best investors occurred within three months of the initial purchase. If you extend the horizon out to six months, a staggering 61% of all profit-taking has occurred.

Only 2% of profits were realised after a holding period of three years or more.

These findings corroborate my general observations that behaviourally many find it hard to hold onto winning investments. It is clear that if you can expand your investment horizon you can have a massive advantage.

3. You cannot trust your next investment

In the introduction to this book I showed that on average only 49% of top investors' ideas made money. Using these odds you might be amazed to know that the chances of investing in five successive winning trades one after another are far worse than 49%. In fact, statistically speaking the odds are less than 2%. This should help reinforce the attraction of sticking with a winning investment when you are itching to sell out and take a small profit!

It is, however, all too easy to be over-confident about reinvesting those profits, especially if you believe you have nothing to lose.

Research by the academics Mike Thaler and Eric Johnson[48] suggests that once a person has sold a winner, his or her behaviour turns from being driven by risk-avoidance to risk-seeking, something they called the *house money* effect. Investors view their profits as 'house money', not their own money. If they lose they feel they haven't really lost anything.

Investors need to try to break the link between success and failure in prior investments if they want to succeed. Always remember:

Selling a winner can seriously damage your wealth.

4. Winners can keep winning

Many studies have shown that momentum investing can be a winning strategy. Stock leadership does seem to persist long enough to exploit it – a greater fool will (almost) always buy at a higher price.

Research by Narasimhan Jegadeesh and Sheridan Titman in 1993 showed that stocks earning relatively high, or low, returns over a three-to-12-month time frame, continued that trend over the subsequent three to 12 months.[49] In other words, winning stocks continued to win (they autocorrelate).

There are many reasons why winners can keep winning. Some researchers suggest that analysts and investors anchor to old and incorrect earnings estimates for a company and are slow to revise their forecasts higher if they are wrong. As they eventually do revise them, this in turn results in a stock being either re-rated or attracting buyers as it surprises – despite nothing fundamentally having changed.

Another possible explanation is a simple bandwagon effect: investors buy winning stocks because that is what the herd is doing. The longer a winning streak goes on, the narrower and narrower the market gets as all the buyers end up moving into the same winning stocks and sectors. Everyone loves a winner and a stock whose share price keeps going up and up becomes a market darling.

Robert Shiller's findings from research he conducted in 1981 suggest that stock prices are driven more by speculators than by company fundamentals.[50] He showed that stock market prices move well beyond what would be predicted by a rational investment model. Quite simply, stock index returns are too volatile relative to aggregate dividends. Indeed, consider the fact that in December 2006, Alan Greenspan, when he was the chairman of the Federal Reserve, publicly declared that markets were being driven higher due to "irrational exuberance". That statement did not stop the stock market going higher for another three years before the bubble eventually popped.

Of course, caution is still required: winners may not win forever. Eventually no marginal buyers are left to bid a stock price higher and a price correction occurs.

5. You can never predict big winners when you first invest

Many legendary investors did not predict their biggest winners – and have admitted it. Some all-time greats even built their investment style around not knowing how big a winner might be: Jesse Livermore became one of the wealthiest men in America in the 20th century by adopting a simple trend-following approach.

In effect he bought stocks that were being bid up and rode them up, never knowing if it would turn out to be a big winner when he initiated the position.

IS IT EVER RIGHT TO SELL A WINNER?

At this point you may be wondering if it can ever be the right thing to sell a winner. It definitely can be. If you know your reason for investing has been proved wrong, then you have no reason to stay invested. You have been lucky and made a profit, but why should you have any conviction that it should persist?

The fact the stock has gone up does not mean you were right any more than a stock going down does not make you wrong *per se*. Recognise you got lucky and sell.

TOO PROFESSIONAL

My findings showed that 68% of the time fund managers took a profit when the stock had relatively outperformed the index by up to 23%. They either had a remarkable natural disposition to avoid big winners – or there were other things going on at the same time. Here are some possible factors slightly unique to professional investors (though everyone can learn from them):

1. Bonuses

Many fund managers are awarded bonuses based on one- and three-year performance relative to a reference index or peer group. When they find themselves in a position of being ahead of that index or peer group, they want to lock in that profit so that they get paid a good bonus at the end of the year.

2. Expectations

Some fund managers I have met will take profits early because they fear the relative outperformance cannot persist. In fact, I have had managers say to me that they have sold out of a stock because they think it will "go to sleep" for the next six months, and as such the capital would be best deployed somewhere else where it can work in the interim. (This overconfidence in their clairvoyant ability to time markets is often their downfall.)

3. Forecasting

Most fund managers invest with a price target in mind that is only 20 to 30% higher than their original purchase price. Part of the reason for this is because they only forecast one to two years out, and only look to be invested in a stock for a short period of time. As a result, many fund managers' processes are not designed to capture big, multi-year winners.

4. Relativity

Finally, many fund managers think in relative terms.

A fund manager's performance is assessed relative to an index or his peers. His or her reviewers (employer and clients) are trying to decide whether the manager has been doing a good job. A comparison with an index is suitable because anyone invested in the fund is paying an active fund manager more than it costs to invest in a passive fund (an index fund or exchange-traded fund) that simply replicates the benchmark. For that extra fee, the client is expecting the fund manager to materially outperform.

A comparison with peers is also fair because the client who has decided that he or she wants to pay for active management could have invested with a number of other active managers.

Many studies over the years have shown that clients have a bias to investing in the best performing funds. Typically, they are funds that are first quartile (ranked in the top 25% of all funds in that space).

So being assessed on a relative basis leads fund managers to pay a *lot* of attention to how they are performing relative to both the benchmark index and their peer group. Worse still, some do this on a daily basis. They know the value of their holdings almost to the hour.

And it leads to a lot of unnecessary early selling. It helps professional investors think that stocks are riskier than they actually are. By monitoring a stock they are invested in several times a day, they notice the share price moves up and down quite a bit. The price seems volatile.

But what if you just reviewed an investment every ten years? You would probably find that the stock has made you quite a lot of money. Moreover, because you did not check the stock price during that ten-year period, you did not notice the price moving up and down every day. You never experienced the pain of a 20% fall in one day – perhaps 50% in a year. You were completely unaware of the volatility of the ride you were on. You therefore come to the conclusion that investing in the stock market is not risky at all.

WHY WAS ONE RAIDER SUCH A SUCCESSFUL HEDGE FUND MANAGER?

Having read this far you might be wondering how the Raider I mentioned at the beginning was such a lousy long-only investor for me but so successful in his day job shorting stocks at a hedge fund.

Funnily enough, the two things go hand in hand. When you short a stock you are looking for the exact opposite in an investment, so this Raider's destructive investment style turned out to be perfectly suited to shorting.

The ruinous policy of cutting his winners and running his losers in investing was the rigorous and prudent policy of running winners and cutting losses when applied to shorting.

When shorting, he sold when a stock rose 10% so as to keep the losses small. When a stock fell in price he rode it down, thus running his winners. In both cases he was getting rid of rising stocks and sticking around with losing ones. I also believe that a key reason it was easier for him to stick with a winning short was that, as it got more profitable, his weight in that stock reduced. The net result being less and less capital was at risk as the short worked.

It's clear that what affected him most profoundly is upside and downside risk. In shorting, the upside is capped at 100% (a stock cannot fall lower than 0) but the downside is potentially infinite (a stock can keep on rising and rising). In investing, the downside is capped at 100% but the upside is potentially infinite.

The former scenario encouraged him to be ruthless with losses and greedy with winners. The latter encouraged him to be indulgent with losses and impatient with winners.

It is obviously worth thinking about how these factors affect you and tailoring your investment approach accordingly – it could be the difference between legendary success and limp failure.

RESISTING THE RAID

In psychology circles there is a famous test in which a marshmallow is placed in front of a young child. The child is told that if he doesn't eat the marshmallow in the next 30 minutes, he will be rewarded with an additional marshmallow.

The researcher then leaves the child alone in a room with the marshmallow sitting in front of him or her on a plate.

There are no distractions. No TV. No music. It is just a room with a kid sitting at a table looking at a marshmallow.

As you might imagine, after just a few minutes most children tend to get fidgety. And in most cases the child succumbs to temptation and shortly thereafter wolfs the marshmallow. Let's face it, half an hour in a room with no toys must feel like 30 years to someone that age.

The point of this test is that it demonstrates a phenomenon known as *inter-temporal choice*. If something is offering us immediate pleasure (like taking profits), we struggle to see the pain it will cause us in the future. We become near-sighted (myopic) and sacrifice potentially large long-term gains for small short-term ones.

Raiders cannot help but eat the whole marshmallow. On the other hand, the final and most successful tribe of investors – the Connoisseurs – have a solution to the marshmallow problem.

5. THE CONNOISSEURS

Enjoying Every Last Drop

The Connoisseurs are the last and most successful investment tribe I discovered among the top investors who worked for me. These are the investors whose performance lived up to the billing – or exceeded it. They did not get paralysed by unexpected losses or carried away with victories. They treated every investment like a vintage of wine: if it was off, they got rid of it immediately, but if it was good they knew that it would only get better with age. They usually drank the odd bottle now and then, to tide them over – but otherwise they sat back and waited.

It takes a lot of nerve to do nothing or merely trim a position when winning. Everything points to us being hard-wired to sell out of an investment when we have made a reasonable profit.

As a professional investor, I can tell you that clients are no different. Having entrusted you with their hard-earned money, they can get seriously annoyed when you persist in holding onto a stock that has made a nice profit. It gets even more awkward if that profit retraces its steps at some point.

Faced with the marshmallow test of the previous chapter, the Connoisseurs had a simple way round it. These investors knew that they could not resist the temptation to eat what was put in front of them. Their strategy was therefore to take a small bite and leave some for later, extending and maximising the pleasure of success as long as possible.

Taking small profits along the journey like a Connoisseur allows us to get instant gratification without ruining our long-term wealth aspirations. This 'trick' is one that I have seen in action and which allowed my best investors to stay in absolutely phenomenal winners.

HOW TO RIDE WINNERS

Many of the Connoisseurs I worked with came across as cerebral, and if you met some you might easily think they became rich by being prodigious thinkers with IQs off the charts.

Don't be fooled. In terms of hit rate, as a group they actually had a *worse* record than the average for my investors. Six out of ten ideas the Connoisseurs invested in lost money. The trick was that when they won, they won big. They rode their winners far beyond most people's comfort zone.

Here's how to be like a Connoisseur, followed by real-life examples of their approach in action:

1. Find unsurprising companies

The Connoisseurs' approach was to identify companies with a view to holding them for ten or more years. They would buy businesses that they viewed as low 'negative surprise' companies. In other words, it was hard to envisage anything that could cause these companies' to fail in generating profits over the years ahead.

Even if in the future they had terrible management at the helm, that management would have to be extraordinarily incompetent to destroy the profit-making ability of the enterprise. The companies were effectively money-printing machines.

The future growth of earnings was seen as very predictable, and because the Connoisseurs believed earnings growth drove stock prices, the stock price should therefore drift higher over time.

The main risk of buying these stocks was if they were rated highly at the outset (i.e. with high price/earnings ratio). This could mean that the company fundamentally performs as expected but the share price doesn't follow earnings upwards due to it getting derated. A stock that the market was willing to pay 25× earnings for today might only trade on 15× its earnings in the future. Value is in the eye of the beholder and at various points the market highly, or lowly, values a company.

2. Look for big upside potential

Given the average success of an investment idea is 49% (and that's the average for some of the very best investors in the world!) it really does matter that when you win, you win big.

Therefore, any investment idea should have very good upside potential. Where many investors go wrong is in investing in too many ideas with limited upside potential (of, say, 10–30%).

This can sometimes be the result of artificial constraints – setting targets far too low, like a Raider. The secret of the Connoisseurs was not only to do away with such unambitious limits (they never used price targets) but also to eschew investments that might only ever perform so modestly. They just weren't interested in small-scale success.

3. Invest big – and focused

When the Connoisseurs were very confident in an idea, they built up big positions. They could end up with 50% of their total assets invested in just two stocks. It was these stocks that made them so successful.

Having massive belief in a couple of names meant they were prepared to ride the stocks with big positions even when they were up 200% or more. Their success was testament to Stanley Druckenmiller's comment that "position size can be more important than entry price."[51]

This is one of the reasons that I allow each of my current investors to invest up to 25% of the money I give them in a single idea.

"When you have tremendous conviction on a trade, you have to go for the jugular. It takes courage to be a pig. It takes courage to ride a profit with huge leverage. As far as Soros is concerned, when you're right on something, you can't own enough."[52]

– New Market Wizards

It is no use having a small investment in a big winner; you have to have a large position size to generate big returns.

4. Don't be scared

One of the keys to riding a big winner is to avoid being scared out of it. The way many Connoisseurs avoided being scared out of a position or being attracted away by another great investment was to take small profits as the stock kept going up rather than selling entirely out of the position having made 20% or 50%.

In other words, lest all the bottles in their cellar got corked, they would take one or two upstairs on special occasions and enjoy them.

5. Make sure you have a pillow

One of the key requirements of staying invested in a big winner is to have (or cultivate) a high boredom threshold.

Meeting some of my Connoisseurs could be very, very boring because nothing ever changed. They would talk about the same stocks they had been invested in for the past five years or longer. On the days I had a meeting scheduled with a Connoisseur, I sometimes struggled to get out of bed.

The fact is, most of us will find it difficult to emulate the Connoisseurs because we feel the need to do something when we get to the office (or home trading desk) every day. We look at stock price charts, listen to the latest market news on Bloomberg TV, and fool ourselves into believing we could add value from making a few small trades here and there. It is very hard to do nothing but focus on the same handful of companies every year, only researching new ideas on the side.

Many of us, seeing we have made a profit of 40% in one of our stocks, start actively looking for another company to invest the money into – instead of leaving it invested. This is precisely why lots of investors never become very successful.

Now let's look at some of the Connoisseurs' real-life investments to see these principles in action:

CASE STUDY: SHOPRITE HOLDINGS

Shoprite Holdings is the largest food retailer in Africa and the chances are, whatever country you visit in Africa, you will come across Shoprite supermarkets. They are even found on the islands of Madagascar and Mauritius.

If you are a wealthy African then in all likelihood you will shop at Checkers, which is Shoprite's high-end hypermarket. If you are at the lower end of the income scale you will probably be a customer of Shoprite Usave.

To give you a feel for just how dominant this company is in Africa, in South Africa they reckon that two out of every three consumers shop at one of Shoprite's supermarkets. Furthermore, this holdings company also owns and operates furniture outlets under the OK brand, fast food outlets under the Hungry Lion brand, and pharmacies under the Medrite brand.

It is rather like the Walmart of Africa; its shops are everywhere.

One of the Connoisseurs decided to invest in Shoprite Holdings on 20 May 2009 when the shares were trading at the sterling equivalent of £3.96 per share. He closed his position three years later on 9 August 2012 with the shares trading at the sterling equivalent of £13.10 per share.

On a buy, hold and do-nothing basis this represented a return of 231% in just three years. As we know, most people have a tendency to sell after making a profit of around 20% or 30%, so most would have given up over 200% by selling too early.

My investor's secret was to take small profits along the way to ensure he stayed invested, a process he would describe as trimming his winners. Like going for a haircut, the idea was to take a little off – not the whole lot. This process meant he didn't quite make the full 231% return, but it did mean that he stayed invested.

In the end he achieved an average selling price of £9.31 per share. This meant he made a profit of 104% – still up to five times what most other investors in that stock would have experienced, given my findings.

CASE STUDY: SPIRAX–SARCO ENGINEERING

Spirax-Sarco is a UK company that helps to build and maintain steam and industrial fluid plants. While few of us will have ever heard of it – it is far from a consumer brand – it is the world leader in the manufacturing of boiler and pipeline control valves, and steam traps for steam heating. It is known for its high standards.

Guinness chose Spirax-Sarco's clean steam generator to help ensure it met strict quality and flavour guidelines in the production of its beer (the clean steam generator basically sterilises kegs).

You might also see Spirax-Sarco's equipment in hospitals, where its cleaning systems have been beneficiaries of energy efficiency drives. For example, Spirax-Sarco's EasiHeat system was recently installed at Stafford General Hospital in the UK because it is more efficient at heating water than the old calorifiers (a water storage vessel that heats water) and should save them more than £3,000 a year in energy bills.

The company stands to benefit significantly from the trend towards doing things in a greener and more cost-efficient manner.

In the food industry, where the trend is towards ready-to-eat products, Spirax-Sarco's steam controls are being used more and more. For example, Moy Park recently installed a new oven in which to cook its ready-to-eat roast chickens. Spirax-Sarco installed a steam control unit that meant, within the oven, steam would humidify and keep the chickens moist.

As you can see, Spirax-Sarco products are everywhere.

Spirax-Sarco is a company that one of the Connoisseurs had known for nearly two decades. He decided to initiate a position in the stock on 30 November 2007, when the shares traded at £9.63 per share. He sold five years later on 22 October 2012 with the shares trading at £19.70 per share. On a buy, hold and do-nothing basis this represented a return of 105%.

This Connoisseur, by staying invested in the stock, but trimming his position and realising small profits along the way, made a handsome return of 70%. By gradually trimming he achieved an average selling price of £16.40 per share. Not bad when you consider most people would probably have sold outright when the shares got to around £11.50 (a 20% profit).

CASE STUDY: ROTORK

Unless you are in the oil, gas, or water industries, Rotork is another company you will never have heard of. It is a UK-based business and the world's leading manufacturer of valve actuators, whether they be electric, pneumatic or hydraulic. It basically provides engineers with dependable solutions to manage the flow of liquids, gases and powders.

Like Spirax, Rotork was a company that a Connoisseur had known for a long time. He initiated a position in the stock on 30 November 2007 when the shares traded at £9.84 per share.[53] He sold five years later on 4 December 2012 with the shares trading at £25.18 per share.

On a buy, hold and do-nothing basis, this represented a staggering return of 156%. My investor's action of taking small profits along the journey meant he achieved an average selling price of £17.26 per share, and that when he sold out completely he made an excellent profit of 74%.

CASE STUDY: PRESIDENT CHAIN STORES

President Chain Stores (PCS) is a Taiwanese company. Many of us will be familiar with its products – just not its name. The company is an international food conglomerate operating in Taiwan and China. Rather like Walmart, it sells everything from own-brand milk and yoghurts to noodles, bread – and more or less anything else you can think of. While you may not be familiar with PCS, you will be familiar with the other stores they operate under licence in Taiwan, such as 7-Eleven, Starbucks, Mister Donut and Carrefour. PCS also owns the Uni-President Lions, a professional baseball team in Taiwan's Chinese Baseball league.

One of the Connoisseurs initiated a position in President Chain Stores on 15 June 2006, which was the day I gave him money to invest. At that point the shares were trading at the equivalent of £1.37 per share. He sold five years later on 23 August 2011 with the shares trading at £3.73 per share. On a buy, hold and do-nothing basis this represented a return of 173%, but given this investor liked to trim his winners the average sell price he achieved was £3.17 per share, which meant that when he eventually sold out completely he had made a profit of 132%.

CASE STUDY: KASIKORNBANK

Kasikornbank is a commercial bank based in Thailand. If you have ever been to Thailand the chances are you will have used one of its ATMs to withdraw money. Through its wholly-owned subsidiaries it does everything from investment banking to securities brokerage, fund management, hire purchase and machinery/equipment leasing. If you read one of its strategy documents you will see that its goal is to be Thailand's main consumer bank.

A Connoisseur initiated a position in Kasikornbank on 20 June 2008 when the shares traded at the equivalent of £1.09 per share. He sold two years later on 1 November 2010 with the shares trading at £2.65 per share. On a buy-and-hold basis this represented a return of 143%, but the investor's trimming meant that his average sell price was £1.88 per share. Thus, when he eventually sold out completely he had made a profit of 79%.

DEALING WITH LOSSES

Remember, despite their successful approach, only one-in-three of the Connoisseurs' ideas made money. In other words, every Connoisseur was also an Assassin or a Hunter when it came to losses.

CLUES FROM THE *FORBES* RICH LIST

Having discovered that one half of the secret to making money, even if we are wrong most of the time, is to ride your winners in size, I now look at the *Forbes* rich list in a new light.

Previously, I would look at it and think, "Why didn't I think of that?" Or, "He must be a genius."

For example, at the time of writing, Jeff Bezos at a relatively youthful age of 49 is ranked as the 18th richest person on the planet, with a net worth of $25bn. That makes him richer than the entire economies of Paraguay and Jamaica.

How did Jeff become so fabulously wealthy?

The popular story told by mainstream media is that he became rich because he founded Amazon, which has grown from being a humble online book store to the world's largest online retailer. The story which is overlooked and never discussed is the fact that he really became super rich because *he had a large stake in Amazon and he never sold out.*

The importance of this simple observation should not be underestimated.

Over the past decade or so, I would imagine Bezos has been approached by hundreds, possibly thousands of other companies wanting to buy Amazon from him. Could you have resisted if someone offered you $10m or $100m for your company? Resisting temptation and staying invested in a great idea is critical. Had Jeff sold out earlier when he was building Amazon, we may never have heard about him today.

Let's take another example. Sara Blakely, at the youthful age of 42, has just joined the ranks of the super rich with a net worth of over $1bn. In fact, she is the youngest self-made female billionaire. What was the secret of her success?

The official line spun by the media is that she is the creator and founder of Spanx, a clothing line that goes under your clothes to help keep the fat tucked away and give you a firmer shape. Some will also tell you she is the embodiment of the American dream, having gone from being a lowly paid employee at Disney World to super rich, because at the age of 29 she took her life savings of $5,000 and invested in herself. She designed, manufactured and sold her clothes from her Atlanta apartment, before opening her own shops in retail malls. Others will say to you she got rich thanks to Oprah Winfrey, because Spanx was named one of 'Oprah's Favorite Things'.

The one thing you do not hear is that she made a lot of money because she stayed invested in her great idea. Even today, at the time of writing, she owns 100% of her company.

When you are winning, dedication and discipline is what you require. The Pareto principle, otherwise known as the 80/20 rule, states that 80% of the effects come from 20% of the causes. It helps explain why great investors can be wrong most of the time and still make money. A few big winners make a massive difference to the eventual outcome.

Take any person on the *Forbes* rich list and the common thread that binds them all is that they have large stakes in a company that they have continued to hold.

WHY MANY FUND MANAGERS ARE DOOMED TO FAIL

Unfortunately, many fund managers find it almost impossible to be Connoisseurs.

Firstly, many professional investors over-diversify when they invest because they are managing their career risk. Most are judged by their bosses and employers based on how they perform against an index or peer group over a *short* period of time. This militates against concentrating investments in potential long-term winners.

Secondly, regulators – based on investment theories from the 1970s – have put into place rules that prohibit professional fund managers from holding large positions in just a handful of their very best money-making ideas.

Why?

Because they believe diversified portfolios represent less risk than a concentrated portfolio of stocks. The reality, however, is that all you are doing is swapping one type of risk for another. You are exchanging company specific risk (idiosyncratic risk), which may be very low depending on the type of company you invest in, for market risk (systematic risk).

Risk hasn't been reduced, it has been transferred.

ACADEMIC SUPPORT FOR 'BEST IDEAS' INVESTING

There is strong academic evidence for why investing in just your highest-conviction ideas makes sense. A paper by professors from Harvard University and the London School of Economics examined the performance of the stocks that represented investment managers' very best ideas (based on holding sizes).[54]

To ensure their findings were robust, they focused on all the US-registered domestic equity funds that filed their quarterly holdings with the Securities Exchange Commission (SEC) over a 14-year period beginning in January 1991 and ending in December 2005. This was a period that captured both the massive technology bubble of the late 1990s and the subsequent popping of that bubble and stock market crash from 2000 to 2002.

Given the fact that it is a requirement for most funds to file their holdings with the SEC, their study captured the majority of funds in existence that people could invest in during that period. The only caveat was that the fund had to have net assets of at least $5m and contain at least 20 stocks. Index funds were excluded for the obvious reason that they try to replicate the performance of an index, and the largest holdings cannot be said to represent an active manager's best ideas.

Their findings were startling. They discovered:

- The single highest-conviction stock of every manager taken together outperformed the market, as well as the other stocks in those managers' portfolios, by approximately 1–14%. That is a staggering 4–16% a year. Over a ten-year time frame, that means these stocks could have outperformed the market by a phenomenal 48–341%!

- The managers' top five stocks also outperformed the market, as well as the other stocks in those managers' portfolios, significantly.

- The managers' worst ideas – those stocks with the lowest weighting[55] – performed significantly worse than the managers' best ideas.

A cynical reviewing of these findings might quickly conclude that the results must be skewed by significant overlap between managers' best ideas, or that maybe there were times when a particular stock was hot and everyone bought it. However, that was not the case. In fact, the findings showed that "more than 70% of best ideas did not overlap across managers ... and only 8% of best ideas overlap over three managers at a time."

This lends support to the notion that success is not determined by luckily investing in the hot stock at any one time. Rather, it is about investing in *your* best idea.

The authors of the paper concluded by posing a simple question:

> "What if each mutual fund manager had only to pick a few stocks, their best ideas? Could they outperform under those circumstances? We document strong evidence that they could, as the best ideas of active managers generate up to an order of magnitude more alpha than their portfolio as a whole."

This research paper shows that professional investors do have skill in picking stocks, especially when it relates to their best ideas. It seems that over-diversification is another thing to blame for poor performance by professional investors.

> "The poor overall performance of mutual fund managers in the past is not due to a lack of stock-picking ability, but rather to institutional factors that encourage them to over diversify, i.e. pick more stocks than their best alpha-generating ideas."

Phrased differently:

> "the organization of the money management industry appears to make it optimal for managers to introduce stocks into their portfolios that are not outperformers ... [in other words] managers attempt to maximise profits by maximizing assets under management ... while investors benefit from concentration ... managers under most commonly-used fee structures are better off with a more diversified portfolio."[56]

DANGERS OF BEING A CONNOISSEUR

As the most profitable form of investing, being a Connoisseur is not easy. Not only does it run against some pretty strong impulses, it also comes with some significant dangers that must be watched for.

There are three in particular:

1. You can be too late

As we covered earlier, Ned Davis, using the Dow Jones Industrial Average Index from 1929 to 1998, showed that the bulk of investors' returns (more or less half) in bull markets come in the first third of a rally.[57] He also showed that the first half of a rally accounts for two-thirds of the overall return in a bull market. This is something to keep in mind if you are buying a winner – the easy money has arguably been made.

The longer a rally has gone on, the greater the likelihood it is nearer to the end than the beginning.

2. Momentum can be illusory – and end abruptly

The longer a stock has been winning, and the more widespread its story has become, the more speculators will have bought into it with the view to own it for as long as the 'trend is their friend'.

Some high-performance stocks should be thought of as viral stocks. The hidden force that drives speculative money to buy into a winner is the same as that which causes us to choose to dine in a restaurant that has a queue coming out of the door. Success has an allure. But not all success will last forever.

Investors seem to be hard-wired to follow the herd, so we need to be careful when riding a winning stock. Charles Mackay, in his 1841 book *Extraordinary Popular Delusions and the Madness of Crowds*, examined three bubbles (the 18th-century Mississippi project, the South Sea bubble, and the 17th-century Dutch tulip mania). His research showed how people lose the ability to think rationally under pressures of crowd behaviour. At the height of a bull market or in the depths of a bear market people become herd-minded. And it is rarely safe to be relying on irrationality for profit for too long.

"I learned that even though markets look their very best when they are setting new highs, that is often the best time to sell. He [Eli Tullis] instilled in me the idea that, to some extent, to be a good trader, you have to be contrarian."[58]
– Paul Tudor Jones II

This suggests that sipping some of those profits over time makes a lot of sense. While you stay invested and therefore have the potential to win big, you are mitigating the potential damage should the shares disappoint.

3. You can get stuck

Ned Davis makes a brilliant point about the danger of crowded trades:[59] if someone yells fire in a theatre filled to the rafters with people, panic breaks out and people can be crushed rushing for the exits. However, if someone yells fire in a theatre with very few people, the people can get up, look for signs of fire, and walk out in an orderly manner.

This is another reason that the Connoisseurs' approach of taking *some* profit over the years is a good idea. It's like inching towards the fire exit.

Sir Isaac Newton famously lost everything with his investment in the South Sea stock in the 1700s. The amazing thing, however, was that he was early into the trade and sold out completely having made a nice profit. Then the stock kept going up, and Newton saw his friends who had remained invested become very rich. So he bought back in, this time with a larger stake. Sadly, it was not far from the top and the stock subsequently collapsed and he was left broke. This led him to say:

"I can calculate the orbit of the heavenly bodies but I cannot fathom the madness of men."

ARE YOU READY TO BE A CONNOISSEUR?

It takes a lot of nerves and patience to be a Connoisseur. It's something everyone should aspire to – but few find easy. Hopefully this chapter has inspired you to join their ranks. My research showed that the best investors all benefited from holding a few massive winners. Strip out these big winners and their returns would be distinctly average.

The reason Steve Jobs became one of the richest men in the world is because he held onto his investment in his company. Could you have held onto shares in Apple from 1984 when they were $3 a share, to 2012 when they were $700?

Would you have been able to take a few bites out of Apple – but not eat it all?

I am not saying you need to be invested for three decades to become rich, but you do need a process that allows you to embrace big winners.

As Stanley Druckenmiller once said:

> "[The] way to build long-term returns is through preservation of capital and home runs. Many managers, once they're up 30 or 40 percent, will book their year … The way to attain truly superior long-term returns is to grind it out until you're up 30 or 40 percent, and then if you have the convictions, go for a 100 percent year."[60]

CONCLUSION
The Habits of Success

Having had the privilege of investing over a billion dollars with the best investors in the world, and managing them on a daily basis for over eight years, my preconceptions about successful investors have been shattered.

I discovered that the success enjoyed by top investors is not due to possessing a special gift, nor from having a privileged upbringing (though some who worked for me did). Nor is it down to being born geniuses, though many were very smart. Instead, any success ultimately came down to just one thing: execution.

This was the common thread that connected all of them. And the secrets of successful execution were really just a matter of habit.

I've divided the investors into tribes or gangs, but the really interesting thing is that almost none of the investors self-identified as any kind of investor when it came down to execution. It was all habit – just what they did.

Each had learned the unseen art of executing ideas in a way that meant that even if they were wrong most of the time, they would still make a lot of money.

These habits meant they did not need to possess a gift that enabled them to buy or sell shares at the right time. They did not need clairvoyant forecasting abilities. The hidden habits meant they knew what to do when they found themselves in a losing situation, and likewise what to do when they found themselves in a winning situation.

If they were losing they knew they had to materially adapt, like a poker player being dealt a poor hand. A losing position was feedback from the market showing them that they were wrong to invest when they did. They knew that doing nothing, or a little, was futile. They had each independently developed a habit of significantly reducing or materially buying more shares when they were losing.

When winning, to take an analogy from baseball, the successful investors knew they had to try to hit a home run, as opposed to stealing first base. This meant that they had developed the hidden habit of being resolved to stay invested in a winning position even when inside they were burning to take the profits they had made, and their inner voice was screaming, "Take the profit before you lose it!"

I realise that some readers might be disappointed that the winning habits I have uncovered are too simple, too basic – nothing new. No doubt some readers will feel I am oversimplifying things, and that to become a good executor of ideas is an art that takes decades to master. The truth is often disappointing when you discover it.

Successful investors want you to think that success in investing is beyond the abilities of the average person. They want you to believe that returns are driven by managers and teams possessing special gifts. This is propaganda. Success in investing is open to anyone, whatever their level of education or background, whether old or young, experienced or inexperienced. You simply need to materially adapt when losing and remain faithful when winning.

If you have the discipline to do that, you can succeed.

I have no doubt that many professional investors reading this will neither change the way they invest nor adopt the winning habits I have revealed. They will consider them too simple or common. Most think they are just too smart and that they know best. They are overconfident in the same way all drivers think they are better than average. It's their loss.

In the spirit of the film *Trading Places*, I wager that I could teach these habits to a kid in secondary school and they would outperform most professional investors today. In fact, I am prepared to offer such a challenge to the CIO of any investment house.

A DINNER TO REMEMBER

Some people may worry that adopting the habits of the successful investing tribes means losing their own identity – or looking to invest with ideas that aren't really theirs. The good news is that the investors within each group all had radically different opinions about almost everything. Their habits of execution overlapped, but the ideas that got them into an investment in the first place could not have been more different.

I will always recall a particularly vivid illustration of this.

In the summer of 2011, on the back of the success of my European Best Ideas fund, I gathered some of my investors for a dinner hosted by my most high-profile investor, the legendary billionaire hedge fund manager, Crispin Odey.

Many things stand out from that evening. But the most striking thing wasn't the fact that we'd managed to get so many top investors from across the world to sit down for dinner together, nor the setting of a fabulous dining room opening out onto a courtyard at the back of Crispin's offices – nor even that Crispin had done something straight out of a Hollywood film and arranged for his friend, the celebrated chef Michel Roux, to cook for us. The food was brought over from the Gavroche restaurant, about ten metres across the road from where we sat. And it was accompanied by wines of a calibre I had never seen before – and probably never shall see again.

The most striking thing was the arguments.

Around the table sat a motley crew of Connoisseurs, Hunters and Assassins – all leading investors of the very highest calibre – and you would struggle to find so many contradictory views among so few people.

There is nothing quite like seeing a couple of investment titans debating the merits of an investment, one of them telling the other that he is insane to even consider the merits of a stock.

You might reasonably assume that one would be a winner and the other a loser; after all, the market is a zero-sum game. Not so. All were successful despite having different and conflicting views about what to invest in, because they all shared the same habits. They had all mastered the art of executing their ideas.

While many factors cause stock prices to rise and fall, the ultimate determinant of whether you will make or lose money is your actions.

"Lots of people know what to do, but few people actually do what they know. Knowing is not enough! You must take action."
– Tony Robinson

"The future depends on what you do today."
– Gandhi

THE WINNER'S CHECKLIST

*The five winning habits
of investment titans*

1. BEST IDEAS ONLY

Invest in just a handful of your very best ideas. My findings show that having one or two big winners is essential for success – the 80/20 rule (the Pareto principle) is true.

> "Why not buy more of your best idea rather than your 60th idea?"
> **– Bruce Berkowitz**

> "Put all your eggs in one basket and then watch that basket."
> **– Mark Twain**

However, I advise against investing in just *one* great idea because, quite simply, bad luck happens. Moreover, my research shows that your chances of success are less than 50%. With such odds, going all in makes no sense.

2. POSITION SIZE MATTERS

Invest a large amount of money in each idea, but not so much that one decision determines your fate. Act like a successful gunslinger, not an arrogant gunslinger.

The arrogant gunslinger decides to load only one bullet into the chamber of his gun because he is so confident in his ability that he believes he will not need the other five bullets.

As he stares down from heaven at his blood-soaked corpse ten minutes later, he realises that the reason successful gunslingers survive to become legends is because they always have fully loaded chambers. They know that, every now and then, they need more than one bullet.

I often refer to the process of adding money to a losing position as firing another bullet. Not having all your capital tied up in one idea means you get multiple opportunities to achieve success. However, do not invest in too many ideas and over-diversify. Rather, be prepared to invest big – just don't go all in on day one.

3. BE GREEDY WHEN WINNING

Run your winners. You need to embrace the possibility of winning big. Embrace the right tail, the statistical long shots, of the distribution curve. Stop trying to make a quick 10 or 20%. Give your investments the possibility of growing into 'ten baggers'.

4. MATERIALLY ADAPT WHEN YOU ARE LOSING

Either add meaningfully to an existing investment or sell out. Both give you the possibility of changing the ultimate outcome. You can turn a loser into a winner. Expect to find yourself in a losing situation, have a plan to materially adapt, and stick to it.

"Any general in the army knows that no plan survives contact with the enemy."
– Helmuth Karl Bernhard Graf von Moltke

"Everyone has a plan until they get punched in the face."
– Mike Tyson

---

5. ONLY INVEST IN LIQUID STOCKS

Make sure any publicly listed investment is liquid enough to enable you to execute your idea. There is nothing worse than knowing what to do, wanting to do it, but being unable to do it.

THE LOSER'S CHECKLIST

*The five losing habits
of most investors*

1. INVEST IN LOTS OF IDEAS

Many professional fund managers invest in low-conviction, low-expected-return ideas, when they seek diversification in their portfolios to reduce risk.

"As a result of over diversification their returns get watered down. Diversification covers up ignorance. Active managers have not done enough research into any of their companies. If managers have 200 positions, do you think they know what is going on at any one of these companies at this moment?"
– Bill Ackman, Pershing Square

"The average mutual fund that holds 150 names goes that far out on the spectrum more for business reasons than for performance reasons. This is a profession where managers focus a lot on the question: what mistake would it take to get me fired? The answer usually centres on underperformance by a

certain amount, so they develop a strategy to
minimize the probability of that outcome."
– Bill Nygren, Oakmark Funds

<hr/>

<hr/>

"Wide diversification, which necessarily
includes investment in mediocre businesses,
only guarantees ordinary results."
– Charlie Munger, Berkshire Hathaway

<hr/>

2. INVEST A SMALL AMOUNT IN EACH IDEA

If you are wrong most of the time, then you not only need
your winners to win big, but you also need to have enough
capital invested in those ideas to ensure they have a material
impact on your overall outcome.

3. TAKE SMALL PROFITS

Many small profits are the ultimate sign of a losing investment
strategy because you are effectively picking up pennies in
front of an oncoming train.

4. STAY IN AN INVESTMENT IDEA AND REFUSE TO ADAPT WHEN LOSING

5. DO NOT CONSIDER LIQUIDITY

Adopt the five winning habits and avoid the five losing ones, and you'll be well on your way to the kind of stock market execution that can build genuine long-term wealth. Good luck!

Lee Freeman-Shor

ENDNOTES

1   *Being Right or Making Money*, by Ned Davis (2000).

2   As quoted in *Ibid*.

3   'Judgment under uncertainty: Heuristics and biases', *Science*, by Amos Tversky and Daniel Kahneman (1974).

4   *Free Radicals: The Secret Anarchy of Science*, by Michael Brooks (2011).

5   *The General Theory of Employment, Interest and Money*, by John Maynard Keynes (1936).

6   *How We Decide*, by Johan Lehrer (2009).

7   'Money: A Bias for the Whole', *Journal of Consumer Research*, by Himanshu Mishra, Arul Mishra and Dhananjay Nayakankuppam (2006).

8   'Denomination Effect', *Journal of Consumer Research*, Priya Raghubir and Joydeep Srivastava (2009).

9   *One Up on Wall Street*, by Peter Lynch and John Rothchild (2000).

10 *The Dhandho Investor*, by Mohnish Pabrai (2007).

11 Quote attributed to Donald Rumsfeld.

12 *Being Right or Making Money*, by Ned Davis (2000).

13   *Ibid.*

14   *Fortune's Formula*, by William Poundstone (2006).

15   **blog.asmartbear.com/ignoring-the-wisdom-of-crowds. html**

16   *The Little Book of Behavioural Investing*, by James Montier (2010).

17   *An Astronaut's Guide to Life on Earth*, by Col. Chris Hadfield (2013). Referring to his first mission where the objective was to construct a docking module on the Russian space station Mir.

18   In *Market Wizards*, by Jack D. Schwager (1990).

19   In *The New Market Wizards*, by Jack D. Schwager (1994).

20   *So Far, So Good*, by Roy R. Neuberger (1997).

21   *The Wisdom of Crowds*, by James Surowiecki (2005).

22   *Predictably Irrational*, by Dan Ariely (2009). "[T]o be a great investor you should have a clear maximum time for the idea to play out."

23   *The Dhandho Investor*, by Mohnish Pabrai (2007).

24   'Gambling with the House Money and Trying to Break Even: The Effects of Prior Outcomes on Risky Choice', *Management Science*, Richard H. Thaler and Eric J. Johnson, (1990). Available at SSRN: **ssrn.com/ abstract=1424076**

25   Lynch (2000).

26   'Prospect Theory: An Analysis of Decision Under Risk', *Econometrica*, by Daniel Kahneman and Amos Tversky (1979).

27   'The disposition effect and underreaction to news,' *The Journal of Finance*, by A. Frazzini (2006).

28   Extract from Warren Buffett's annual letter to the shareholders of Berkshire Hathaway, (1993).

29 Pabrai (2007).

30 In nominal terms. In real terms after inflation you would hope that this has retained and hopefully increased the purchasing power of the $1,000 invested over that period of time.

31 'Evershed: New Star Property ad campaign lost investors millions', *Investment Week* (2011).

32 'Subjective probability: A judgment of representativeness', by Daniel Kahneman and Amos Tversky in *Judgement Under Uncertainty* by Kahneman, Slovic, Tversky (1972).

33 'Bystander intervention in emergencies: Diffusion of responsibility', *Journal of Personality and Social Psychology*, J. M. Darley and B. Latané (1968).

34 Lynch (2000).

35 *Ibid.*

36 'Some Empirical Evidence on Dynamic Inconsistency', *Economic Letters*, by Richard Thaler (1981).

37 'Anomalies: Intertemporal Choice', *Journal of Economic Perspectives*, George Loewenstein and Richard H. Thaler (1989).

38 'Risk Aversion or Myopia? Choices in Repeated Gambles and Retirement Investments', *Management Science*, by Shlomo Benartzi and Richard Thaler (1999). They showed that the pain of a short-term loss overpowers the pleasure of a long-term gain. This myopic (short-term) focus and a hatred of losing is what Thaler and Benartzi called myopic loss aversion.

39 'Online Investors: Do the Slow Die First?', *EFA*, by Brad Barber and Terrance Odean (1999).

40 'Trading is hazardous to your wealth: the common stock investment performance of individual investors', *The Journal of Finance*, by Brad Barber and Terrance Odean (2000).

41 Kahneman and Tversky (1979).

42 'Focusing on the Forgone: How Value Can Appear So Different to Buyers and Sellers', *Journal of Consumer Research*, by Ziv Carmon and Dan Ariely (2000).

43 *The Psychology of Finance*, by Lars Tvede (1999).

44 *More Than You Know*, by Michael Mauboussin (2006).

45 Mauboussin (2006).

46 *Mean Genes*, by Terry Burnham and Jay Phelan (2001).

47 Lynch (2000).

48 Thaler and Johnson (1990).

49 'Returns to Buying Winners and Selling Losers: Implications for Stock Market Efficiency', *Journal of Finance*, by Narasimhan Jegadeesh and Sheridan Titman (1993).

50 'Do Stock Prices Move Too Much to Be Justified by Subsequent Changes in Dividends?', *American Economic Review*, by Robert Shiller (1981).

51 Druckenmiller is a very famous investor who achieved compounded returns of ~30% from 1986 to 2010 before announcing he was returning all outside investor capital from his Duquesne fund and forming a family office.

52 Schwager (1994).

53 Those of you with a keen eye will note that this was the same date as for Spirax-Sarco. The reason is simple. That's when I gave him the money to invest.

54 'Best Ideas', by Randolph Cohen, Christopher Polk, Bernhard Silli (2010). Available at SSRN: **ssrn.com/abstract=1364827**

55 Active weight, not absolute weight.

56 Cohen, Polk and Silli (2010). Combining several quotes relating to Berk and Green's 2004 findings in their paper: 'Mutual fund flows and performance in rational markets', *Journal of Political Economy*, by Jonathan Berk and Richard Green (2004).

57 Davis (2000).

58 Quoted in Schwager (1990).

59 Davis (2000).

60 Schwager (1994).

INDEX

S

THANKS
FOR READING!

Our readers mean everything to us at Harriman House. As a special thank-you for buying this book let us help you save as much as possible on your next read:

If you've never ordered from us before, get £5 off your first order at **harriman-house.com** with this code: aofe51

Already a customer? Get £5 off an order of £25 or more with this code: aofe25

Get 7 days' FREE access to hundreds of our books at **volow.co** – simply head over and sign up.

Thanks again!
from the team at

Codes can only be used once per customer and order. T&Cs apply.

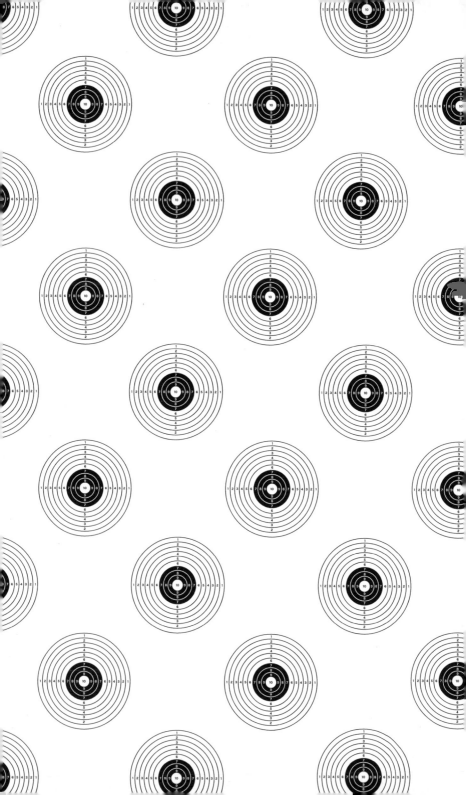